EQUAL UNDER THE LAW

How God's Law Establishes Equal Rights for All

Jaród Murphey

GLASS MOUNTAINS
PUBLISHERS

Glass Mountains Publishers
820 W Danforth Rd
Unit #476
Edmond, OK 73003

ISBN: 979-8-9933099-8-9

Dedicated to my beloved miscarried child, “Bean,”
who is now safe in the arms of God.

Table of Contents

INTRODUCTION

Do humans have objective, inviolable rights? If so, where do these rights come from? What are these rights? And, are human rights truly equal? These are some of the most fundamental questions to ask in order to create just laws. This book will answer all of them.

The first question is relatively easy to answer. It is absurd to deny that humans have at least some objective moral rights that are universal and timeless, unchanging with culture. Was it objectively wrong for Black people to be enslaved in the South, in violation of their basic human right to not be owned as property by anyone else? Was it objectively wrong for the Nazis to murder the Jews in the Holocaust, in violation of their basic human right to life? Or was it acceptable because these actions were condoned by the culture at the time? If you lived in a nation that decided your race was subhuman and proceeded to take away your daughters as sex slaves and murder every other member of your race, including you, would they be violating any timeless, objective human rights?

The answers to these questions are obvious. Someone who says that a child does not have a universal right, applicable across all time periods and cultures, to not be raped, tortured, and brutally murdered is just as wrong as someone who says that one plus two equals five. All humans, except possibly for some diagnosed mental incompetents, have an intuitive awareness that objective moral duties and human rights exist, just as they are aware that the realm of objective mathematics exists. Two plus two never ceases to equal four and a child never loses the right to not be raped and murdered, regardless of what any person, government, or society believes.

Unfortunately, however, people are just as terrible at getting moral truth and human rights correct as they are at mathematics. So who is to say what the objective standard is when it comes to human rights? One society says that Black people have the right to not be enslaved, while another says that they don't. One state says that pre-born humans have a right to life, while another denies this right exists. One person says that women have a right to vote, while another vehemently disagrees. Who is to say what is right?

In the next chapter of this book, I will build the case that the Law of God is the only objective foundation for moral duties and rights which are applicable to individuals, societies, nations, and governments. Chapter I will help you understand God's Law so that you will know how to apply it. Subsequent chapters in this book will then examine specific human rights which are protected by God's Law. Although there are many human rights guaranteed by the Law of God which are not discussed in this book, I selected the rights believed to be of particular relevance to the issues faced by twenty-first century Western societies.

This book will likely offend both right-wingers and left-wingers, as both these political extremes in the West have broken the Law of God and denied basic human rights to certain classes of God's image bearers. As you read what God expects in His Law in regards to human rights, it is critical to not elevate partisan loyalties above what God has plainly commanded, effectively making political parties into idols. Deuteronomy 28:14 warns,

> …Do not turn aside from any of the words which I command you today, to the right or to the left, to go after other gods to serve them.

We must repent of making right-wing or left-wing political affiliations into our gods and, instead, seek wisdom and direction from God's Word. God alone must be our highest loyalty. Proverbs 4:20-27 beautifully illustrates this truth:

> My son, give attention to my words; incline your ear to my sayings. Do not let them depart from your sight; keep them in the midst of your heart. For they are life to those who find them and health to all their body. Watch over your heart with all diligence, for from it flow the springs of life. Put away from you a deceitful mouth and put devious speech far from you. Let your eyes look directly ahead and let your gaze be fixed straight in front of you. Watch the path of your feet and all your ways will be established. Do not turn to the right nor to the left; turn your foot from evil.

CHAPTER 1

DISPENSATIONAL THEONOMY

Before we look at specific human rights which are protected by God's Law, it is first critical to understand what the Law is and how to apply it, the study of which is known as *theonomy* (the Greek word for the "Law of God"). At this point, you may be asking some important questions: why is it necessary for a nation to ground its rights and its laws in the Law of God? Isn't it better for a nation to base these things on secular and cultural values? And what exactly does the Law of God refer to? If a nation enforces the entire Law of God found in the Bible, wouldn't that mean Sabbath-breaking and eating pork would be made illegal? This chapter will answer each of these questions and will present the case that nations should obey the Law of God.

THE ROLE OF CIVIL GOVERNMENT

Romans 13:1-5 says the following about the purpose of civil governments:

> Every person is to be in subjection to the governing authorities. For there is no authority except from God, and those which exist are established by God. Therefore whoever resists authority has opposed the ordinance of God; and they who have opposed will receive condemnation upon themselves. For rulers are not a cause of fear for good behavior, but for evil. Do you want to have no fear of authority? Do what is good and you will have praise from the same; for it is a minister of God to you for good. But if you do what is evil, be afraid; for it does not bear the sword for nothing; for it is a minister of God, an avenger who brings wrath on the one who practices evil.

According to this passage, the God-ordained purpose of civil government is to serve those who do good and bring wrath and vengeance on those who do evil. How should governments determine what is good, evil, or what rights God has given to man? Non-Christians have a variety of sources for grounding civil laws and human rights, such as Sharia Law or cultural values. For a Christian, there can be only one answer: there is no other foundation for just civil law, which includes equal rights for all humans, than the Law of God. Without this presupposition, chaos ensues.

A true Christian loves the Law of God and recognizes the value of applying it in all areas of life. Psalm 19:7-8 comments,

> The law of the Lord is perfect, restoring the soul; the testimony of the Lord is sure, making wise the simple. The precepts of the Lord are right, rejoicing the heart; the commandment of the Lord is pure, enlightening the eyes.

If civil law is not based on the Law of God, it will be imperfect; its foundation will be unsure; it will not be right; and it will not be pure. In proportion to the degree a government strays from legislating according to the Law of God, it can expect its people to be oppressed and miserable; its leaders to be fools; and its institutions to be filled with confusion and turbulence.

PRESUPPOSING THE LAW OF GOD

A great scholar of theonomy, R.J. Rushdoony, wrote the following in his book *By What Standard?*

> Basic to this study is the belief that the presuppositions of human thought in every field must be basically one in order to arrive at any concept which both validates biblical faith and human knowledge. The sovereignty of the self-contained God is the key to every field, in that only the God of Scripture makes all things possible and explicable and is thus the basic premise not only of theology, but of philosophy, science and indeed all knowledge. In that God is the Creator of all things, He is their only valid principle of interpretation, in that they derive both their existence and meaning from His creative act.[1]

Intuitively, most Christians recognize the truth and necessity of presupposing God's existence and authority

---

[1] Rushdoony, R. (1958). *By What Standard? An Analysis of the Philosophy of Cornelius Van Til.* Pg. VII. Ross House Books.

in every area. If you ask a Christian why murder should be outlawed, he will (hopefully) answer, "Because God says murder is wrong," and he will be right in saying this.

If, on the other hand, laws should be based on cultural preferences, there is no reason to say the laws in the South which permitted chattel slavery were wrong, since maintaining this system was the preference of Southern culture. If laws should be based on some notion of "human flourishing" driven by societal evolution, then there is no basis to condemn the atrocities of the Nazis, who were creating a more genetically-perfect human race by exterminating the disabled and those they deemed genetically inferior, like Jews.

If laws should be based on some religion other than Christianity, which one? In accordance with Islamic law, should wife-beating (Surah An-Nisa 4:34) and the marriage of adult men to six-year-old girls, with sexual consummation of the marriage at the age of nine (Sahih al-Bukhari 5134), be permitted? Should a societal caste arrangement (which forces millions into poverty with no hope of escape) be implemented, in accordance with the Hindu Varna system as required under the Laws of Manu?

Should the government require or tolerate sacrificing war captives, poor people, women, children, and babies to appease the gods, in accordance with many pagan religions, like those of the Canaanite, Aztec, Inca, and Maya civilizations? To avoid genocide, the violation of human rights, and utter insanity, a Christian recognizes that a nation must base its laws and rights on the objective foundation of the Law of God as revealed in the Bible.

Since "theonomy" is the Law of God, a "theonomist" is someone who desires to obey and implement, in all areas of his influence, the Law of God, which includes the protection of his neighbors' God-given rights. The area of a theonomist's influence may include family, church, business, nation, government, etc. As Rushdoony put it,

> The man who is being progressively sanctified will inescapably sanctify his home, school, politics, economics, science, and all things else by understanding and interpreting all things in terms of the word of God and by bringing all things under the dominion of Christ the King.[2]

---

[2] Bahnsen, G. (2002). *Theonomy in Christian Ethics*. Pg. XII. Covenant Media Press.

This sanctification process which Rushdoony speaks of is accomplished by the grace of God and the power of the Holy Spirit, with the end goal of enabling us to perfectly and joyfully obey the Law of God. Greg Bahnsen, another scholar of theonomy, adds,

> The Christian is obligated to keep the whole law of God as a pattern of sanctification, and in the realm of human society the civil magistrate is responsible to enforce God's law against public crime.[3]

Has the Law Been Abolished?

A foundational scripture in support of theonomy is Matthew 5:17-19, where our Lord pronounces,

> Do not think that I came to abolish the Law or the Prophets; I did not come to abolish but to fulfill. For truly I say to you, until heaven and earth pass away, not the smallest letter or stroke shall pass from the Law until all is accomplished. Whoever then annuls one of the least of these

[3] Ibid, pg. XXXIX.

> commandments, and teaches others to do the same, shall be called least in the kingdom of heaven; but whoever keeps and teaches them, he shall be called great in the kingdom of heaven.

Unfortunately, very few Christians recognize the importance of this passage because of an assumption about what it meant for Jesus to "fulfill" the Law and the Prophets. Many people believe that Jesus fulfilled the Law and the Prophets by obeying the commands found in them perfectly (which is true) and that Christ has imputed His righteousness to us (which is also true), and therefore we do not have to obey God's Law (which is *not* true). A much better understanding of "fulfill" is offered by John MacArthur in his commentary on this passage:

> …Jesus fulfilled the Old Testament by *being* its fulfillment. He did not simply teach it fully and exemplify it fully—He was it fully. He did not come simply to teach righteousness and to model righteousness; He came as divine righteousness. What He said and what He did reflected who He is.[4]

[4] MacArthur, J. (1985). *The MacArthur New Testament Commentary: Matthew 1-7*. Pg. 256. Moody Publishers.

As the fulfillment of the Law and Prophets, it would be nonsensical for Jesus to abolish them. Thus, every detail of the Law and the Prophets remain in effect "until heaven and earth pass away." Furthermore, Christians are solemnly warned not to "annul one of the least of these commandments;" rather, they are admonished to fully keep the commandments and teach others to do the same. Even in the New Testament, we are told in passages like 1 John 3:4 that "sin is lawlessness" and, according to Matthew 7:21-23, that fake Christians will be removed from Christ's presence on the Day of Judgement because He never knew them and because they were those "who practice lawlessness."

We are instructed to be like Christ (1 John 2:6 and 1 Corinthians 11:1). Since Jesus obeyed the commandments of God perfectly and *is* the righteousness of God, we must strive to obey His commandments (1 John 2:3-5, 3:24, and 5:3) and be perfectly righteous (Matthew 5:48). As Jesus asks in Luke 6:46, "Why do you call Me, 'Lord, Lord,' and do not do what I say?"

THE HOLY SPIRIT'S ROLE

At this point, you may be concerned that theonomists promote works-based salvation. This is not the case. A theonomist believes that a Christian can be saved only by grace through faith. But, according to James 2:17, "faith, if it has no works, is dead, being by itself." If someone claims to be a Christian, but does not do good works, his faith is dead and his salvation is not real. Saving faith is manifested in righteous works. And how do Christians know what righteous works are? How do Christians know how to be righteous in their families, in their workplaces, and in their nations?

According to John 16:7-8, the Holy Spirit is responsible for "convict[ing] the world concerning sin and righteousness and judgment." Although the Holy Spirit can use many different methods to convict us of sin and righteousness, probably the most common tool He uses is the Word of God. 1 Timothy 3:16-17 states,

> All Scripture is inspired by God and profitable for teaching, for reproof, for correction, for training in

righteousness; so that the man of God may be adequate, equipped for every good work.

Not only does "all Scripture" include the commandments of Jesus found in the New Testament, it also includes the commandments that He gave as a part of the Law in the Old Testament. Psalm 119:105 says, "Your word is a lamp to my feet and a light to my path." Since the Word includes the Law, it can rightly be stated that the Law of God is a lamp to our feet and a light to our path.

The Law is not found only in the Word of God; it has also been written in the hearts of all men (Romans 2:15). Men know that it is wrong to violate the rights of their neighbors by murdering them, stealing from them, or showing partiality against them, and therefore are without excuse if they disobey God's Law in these areas.

TWO VIEWS OF THEONOMY

The preceding paragraphs presented a rough sketch of the essential foundation of theonomy; but, for those who are interested in a deep study of this area, the books *Theonomy in Christian Ethics* by Greg Bahnsen and *The Institutes of Biblical Law* by R.J. Rushdoony are highly recommended. Although most theonomists will agree on this foundation, there is some diversity of thought regarding how the Law should be interpreted and practically applied today. The two most popular views on theonomy are the Reconstructionist view and the General Equity view. After briefly describing these two views, I will present the case for a new view, Dispensational theonomy.

The most common understanding of Old Testament Law among Christian theologians is that it should be divided into three categories: the moral law, the civil law (also called the judicial law), and the ceremonial law. Historically, most theologians have argued that the moral law is the only part of the Law still relevant today. It is typically asserted that the moral law consists only of the Ten Commandments. These theologians believe the civil law and the ceremonial law are no longer relevant to Christians. They posit that the civil law consisted of rules which were applicable only to the society and culture in ancient Israel. Furthermore, they believe that ceremonial laws (which includes feasts and festivals, dietary restrictions, cleanliness laws, and sacrifices for sins) were fulfilled and abolished after the crucifixion of Christ.

Reconstructionist and General Equity theonomists both disagree with this mainstream understanding of the Law. They correctly point out that the Israelites had no concept of a division between the moral and civil law. Furthermore, to anyone today who reads the Books of the Law without modern theological presuppositions, to impose this division would seem highly arbitrary. To the open-minded reader of the Old Testament, the entire Law appears to be effective forever. Reconstructionist and General Equity theonomists would agree with the standard view of the law in regards to the ceremonial law. They believe it should be divided from the moral and civil law, that it was fulfilled in Christ, and that it is no longer relevant to Christians.

Reconstructionist and General Equity theonomists differ, however, in how they believe theonomy should be applied today. Reconstructionism, the older school of thought, was first made popular in the mid-1900's by the renowned scholars Greg Bahnsen, R.J. Rushdoony, and Gary North. Reconstructionists believe the Law found in the Old Testament should be applied literally to society today. According to this view, the Law is a blueprint for reconstructing any nation which has strayed from God and for establishing the Kingdom of God on earth. So, when Deuteronomy 22:8 says, "When you build a new house, you shall make a parapet for your roof, so that you will not bring bloodguilt on your house if anyone falls from it," a Reconstructionist would argue that this law should be applied today in the exact way it says: nations should have laws today that require new houses to have parapets for their roofs, just like in ancient Israel.

General Equity theonomists, on the other hand, attempt to apply the "intention" or the "spirit" of the Law to today's society. For the General Equity theonomist, the application of the previous verse today would be for a nation to make laws which require roofs, decks, and balconies to have parapets. The spirit of this law dictates that it is evil to have a commonly-accessed high place on your property without a safeguard to keep unsuspecting people from falling and getting hurt or dying. In ancient Israel, people routinely went on top of their roofs and did not usually have decks or balconies; today, it is much more common for people to have a deck or balcony at their house instead of roof-top access. Thus, modern laws should apply to decks and balconies as well. Because General Equity theonomy is more versatile than Reconstructionism, it is the most widely-held view of theonomy today.

What About the Ceremonial Law?

The major weakness of Reconstructionist and General Equity theonomy is their understanding of the ceremonial law. Reconstructionist and General Equity theologians correctly point out the lack of a clear distinction between the moral and the civil law in the Law of God found in the Old Testament and that such distinctions are arbitrary. However, after saying this, they attempt to divide the ceremonial law from the moral and civil law. No unbiased reader of the Old Testament would come to this conclusion. In Deuteronomy 12:28, for example, Moses concludes a list of ceremonial law commands and indicates that these laws should be obeyed "forever," when he says,

> Be careful to listen to all these words which I command you, so that it may be well with you and your sons after you forever, for you will be doing what is good and right in the sight of the LORD your God.

Exodus 31:16-17 states,

> So the sons of Israel shall observe the sabbath, to celebrate the sabbath throughout their generations as a perpetual covenant. It is a sign between Me and the sons of Israel forever; for in six days the LORD made heaven and earth, but on the seventh day He ceased from labor, and was refreshed.

Some theonomists argue sabbath-keeping is a moral law. However, its constant connection with the nation of Israel and the fact that the Bible records no pagan nation ever being punished for refusing to keep the sabbath indicates that it is more likely than not a ceremonial law. If that is the case, it is another example of a ceremonial law that lasts forever.

Regarding the placing of blood on a home's doorpost for Passover (an undisputed ceremonial command), Exodus 12:24 says, "And you shall observe this event as an ordinance for you and your children forever." When speaking about the Day of Atonement, Leviticus 16:29 states,

> This shall be a permanent statute for you: in the seventh month, on the tenth day of the month, you shall humble your souls and not do any work, whether the native, or the alien who sojourns among you.

Additionally, in regards to a ritual purification law, Numbers 19:21 says,

> So it shall be a perpetual statute for them. And he who sprinkles the water for impurity shall wash his clothes, and he who touches the water for impurity shall be unclean until evening.

Theonomists correctly point out that it is illogical to say Jesus' fulfillment of the Law means we no longer have to obey it, but contradict themselves by using this very reasoning to explain why we don't have to obey the ceremonial law. I do not argue that Christians must obey the ceremonial law today; however, this treatment of the ceremonial law shows something is off with how Reconstructionist and General Equity theonomists view the Law. Although these views present an understanding of the Law which is a vast improvement from the traditional approach, they both still miss the mark.

A THIRD OPTION

Instead of Reconstructionist and General Equity theonomy, I propose a new theory of theonomy referred to as Dispensational theonomy. This theory proposes that there are only two laws universally applicable to all of humanity and from which all other laws are derived: love God, and love your neighbor (Matthew 22:37-40). These two laws are objective and universal. But the way these two laws are expressed *sometimes* varies depending on the time period, culture, and dispensation you find yourself living in, in addition to the covenant relationship you and your nation have with God.

To show how Dispensational theonomy should be understood practically, consider an example of primary importance and relevance, the Law of Moses. The Law of Moses was given only to the nation of Israel, not to other nations (Exodus 19 and Deuteronomy 29). This Law contains elements unique to the Israelites, due to their covenant relationship with God. For instance, the Israelites were expected to observe the Sabbath as a sign of this relationship. Exodus 31:13-14 states,

> But as for you, speak to the sons of Israel, saying, "You shall surely observe My sabbaths; for this is a sign between Me and you throughout your generations, that you may know that I am the LORD who sanctifies you. Therefore you are to observe the sabbath, for it is holy to you. Everyone who profanes it shall surely be put to death; for whoever does any work on it, that person shall be cut off from among his people."

To modern-day Christians who do not understand the significance of Israel's covenant relationship to God, the punishment for Sabbath-breaking sounds intense. However, since the Sabbath is a sign of the covenant relationship between God and the people of Israel, infractions are deadly serious. An analogy may help drive this point home: it is not immoral to remove a ring from your finger and throw it to the ground. By itself, such an action has no inherent significance. But if a married woman who is having an argument with her husband removes her wedding ring and throws it to the ground, this action will be significant and painful to her husband; maybe just as painful as if the woman thrust a knife into him. Why? It is just a ring after all. But the reason this action is significant and painful is because the ring is a sign of the marriage covenant between the husband and wife. In the same way, when an Israelite forsook observing the Sabbath, it was a sign that he had forsaken the covenant between Israel and God.

This is one of the reasons why Christians are not required to obey much of the Law of Moses—specifically, the ceremonial laws. Indeed, the entirety of the Law of Moses was meant solely for the Israelites and their descendants for eternity. But laws which are universally applicable to all humanity are included in the Law of Moses. For instance, adultery, bestiality, incest, and child sacrifice are all forbidden in Leviticus 18. After these and other sins are listed, verses 24-25 say,

> Do not defile yourselves by any of these things; for by all these the nations which I am casting out before you have become defiled. For the land has become defiled, therefore I have brought its punishment upon it, so the land has spewed out its inhabitants.

This passage clearly shows it is against the Law of God for both Israelites and Gentiles to commit these wicked acts. Gentile nations were punished in the Old Testament (and are still punished today) for violations of these laws which were universally applicable to all nations. Naturally, they were repeated in the Law of Moses for the people of Israel.

However, there is no record of a Gentile nation being punished for violating the so-called "ceremonial" laws found in the Law of Moses. Sometimes, in the Law of Moses, Gentiles were even specifically exempted from having to follow the same rules given to the Jews. In Deuteronomy 14:21, for instance, the Jews were forbidden to eat animals which had died of natural causes, although foreigners were allowed to. In contrast to the Gentiles, the Jews were punished for violations of these ceremonial laws, the best example being their seventy years of captivity for refusing to keep the sabbatical years (2 Chronicles 36:21).

THE LAW AND THE CHURCH

As mentioned previously, the Law of Moses was given to the Israelites forever and it was never intended primarily for the Gentiles. So, if that is the case, are Messianic Jews (Christians who are Jews) still obligated to obey the Law of Moses? Verses like Hebrews 8:13 and Ephesians 2:15 make it clear that the Law of Moses and the Old Covenant are obsolete for those in Christ.

It is important to note here that these references are to the Old Covenant made with the Israelites during the time of Moses (what is spoken of, for instance, in Deuteronomy 4:13). The Covenant made with Abraham on the other hand (Genesis 12:1-3 and 15:18-20), is not obsolete. As a part of this Covenant, God will give Abraham as many descendants as there are stars in the sky and, according to Genesis 15, they will possess all of the land between the Nile River in Egypt and the Euphrates

River in Iraq, which has not come to pass yet. Furthermore, Romans 11:17 and Ephesians 2:12-13 make it clear that everyone in the Church, including Gentiles, have been grafted in and inherit the promises of this Covenant with Abraham alongside the physical descendants of Abraham, who have not been forsaken from the Covenant. Romans 11:29 states that "the gifts and calling of God are irrevocable," so this covenant with Abraham is not obsolete.

So how is it that the Mosaic Old Covenant and Law of Moses, which last forever, have been made obsolete? Romans 7:1-6 explains how this works:

> Or do you not know, brethren (for I am speaking to those who know the law), that the law has jurisdiction over a person as long as he lives? For the married woman is bound by law to her husband while he is living; but if her husband dies, she is released from the law concerning the husband. So then, if while her husband is living she is joined to another man, she shall be called an adulteress; but if her husband dies, she is free from

> the law, so that she is not an adulteress though she is joined to another man.
>
> Therefore, my brethren, you also were made to die to the Law through the body of Christ, so that you might be joined to another, to Him who was raised from the dead, in order that we might bear fruit for God. For while we were in the flesh, the sinful passions, which were aroused by the Law, were at work in the members of our body to bear fruit for death. But now we have been released from the Law, having died to that by which we were bound, so that we serve in newness of the Spirit and not in oldness of the letter.

In this passage and in Galatians 2:19, Paul makes it clear that because we have died in Christ, who perfectly obeyed the Law, we are no longer bound to it, whether we are Jew or Gentile. It is not that God has revoked the Mosaic Law or Covenant (God cannot go back on His covenants, which are eternal). Instead, believers have died to this law and this covenant and been joined to a New Covenant.

What is this New Covenant, which is referenced in Matthew 26:28, Hebrews 8:13, and Hebrews 10:15-17? The New Covenant was promised to Israel in Jeremiah 31:31-34:

> "Behold, days are coming," declares the Lord, "when I will make a new covenant with the house of Israel and with the house of Judah, not like the covenant which I made with their fathers in the day I took them by the hand to bring them out of the land of Egypt, My covenant which they broke, although I was a husband to them," declares the Lord. "But this is the covenant which I will make with the house of Israel after those days," declares the Lord, "I will put My law within them and on their heart I will write it; and I will be their God, and they shall be My people. They will not teach again, each man his neighbor and each man his brother, saying, 'Know the Lord,' for they will all know Me, from the least of them to the greatest of them," declares the Lord, "for I will forgive their iniquity, and their sin I will remember no more."

Although this New Covenant was made with Israel and will be fulfilled in its entirety in the future when all Israel will be saved (Romans 11:26), it applies now to all those who are in Christ, including Gentiles (Galatians 3:27-28). Unlike the Old Covenant and the Law of Moses which could not produce righteousness in those who heard it and instead only condemned them (Romans 3:19-20 and Romans 4:15), in the New Covenant, the Holy Spirit writes the Law of God on the hearts of those who believe in God. More importantly, the Holy Spirit empowers them to obey it (Galatians 5:22-23).

What is this Law, which is written on our hearts? It is the Two Commandments found in Matthew 22:36-40 (love God with all your heart, soul, and mind, and love your neighbor as yourself), as well as a New Commandment which shows how the Two Commandments should be applied for New Covenant people. The New Commandment is described in John 13:34-35, which says:

> A new commandment I give to you, that you love one another, even as I have loved you, that you

also love one another. By this all men will know that you are My disciples, if you have love for one another.

This New Commandment is also likely referred to as the "Law of Christ" by the Apostle Paul, who makes mention of it in 1 Corinthians 9:21 and Galatians 6:2. Just like the "ceremonial law" of the Old Covenant did not apply to those outside the Covenant, this New Commandment does not apply to those outside the New Covenant. Unbelievers are not expected to love each other as Christ loves them. This Commandment serves as a sign for those who are in the New Covenant, allowing everyone to see that those who obey it are part of the New Covenant. In this way, the New Commandment fulfills the same role as sabbath-keeping in the Old Covenant.

ORDINANCES UNIQUE TO THE NEW COVENANT

Similarly, the New Covenant includes various ordinances those outside of the Covenant are not required to keep. Some examples include baptism (Matthew 28:19,

Acts 2:38, and Acts 18:8), communion (Luke 22:19-20 and 1 Corinthians 11:23-26), and gathering together with the saints (Hebrews 10:25). No one who is outside the New Covenant is expected to obey these commands and there is no record in the New Testament of anyone outside the Covenant being punished for not keeping these commands.

However, there is record of punishment on Christians who do not properly observe these ordinances. In 1 Corinthians 11:20-34, for instance, Paul described how certain believers had "fallen asleep" (a term which is only used to describe the death of believers) because they had taken communion in an unworthy manner. This calls to mind the extreme punishments for those who broke the sabbath. In both cases, violations of these commands are an affront to the Covenant made between God and His people.

MUST CHRISTIANS FORSAKE THE OLD TESTAMENT LAW?

A quick note must be added about the Old Covenant before moving on, to avoid placing unnecessary guilt on believers who freely choose to observe ceremonial aspects of the Law of Moses. Some Christians are Messianic Jews who observe Jewish holidays, dietary restrictions, or other elements of the ceremonial law. Although we are dead to the Law of Moses, Romans 14 makes it perfectly clear that it is permissible for believers to still observe the ceremonial law. Furthermore, if their conscience requires them to, it would be sinful if they did not. According to the same passage, believers who observe these laws should not condemn those who don't; and those who do not observe them should not despise those who do (Romans 14:10).

Additionally, some believers (both Jews and Gentiles) love and rejoice in the Jewish origins of Christianity and freely choose to celebrate some Jewish holidays or otherwise partake in Jewish culture. There is nothing wrong with this. If Jesus celebrated the Festival of Dedication, Hanukkah (John 10:22-23), it is fine for you to as well. Since the celebration of Hanukkah is not mentioned in the Old Testament—as it was invented after the canon had been completed—we can infer that there is nothing inherently wrong with a Christian celebrating extra-Biblical Jewish festivals in addition to the Biblical ones. Anyone who condemns you for doing this is also condemning the actions of their Savior, who participated in these activities. Similarly, if Paul participated in Jewish purification rituals after the death and resurrection of Christ and after he became a Christian (Acts 21:20-24), you can too. Anyone who condemns you for doing this also condemns the actions of Paul.

YOU HAVE REACHED YOUR DISPENSATION

Returning to the main subject of this study, the application of the Two Commandments can vary depending on the dispensation that you live in. According to C.I. Scofield, one of the first authors to popularize the Biblical study of dispensationalism, "A dispensation is a period of time during which man is tested in respect to obedience to some *specific* revelation of the will of God."[5]

During the 4,000 years between the Fall and the death and resurrection of Jesus, mankind was directed to make animal sacrifices as a test of their obedience and love for God, and to look forward to the future sacrifice of Christ. During this dispensation, the Two Commandments were applied by offering animal sacrifices, even outside the Covenants and the Law of Moses. Abel and Job, for instance, both made animal sacrifices even though they did not have the Law of Moses and were not part of the Abrahamic or Mosaic covenants. However, in this present dispensation after the sacrifice of Christ, God does not expect or desire humanity to offer animal sacrifices. But, in the dispensation that will begin with the return of Christ, animal sacrifices will again be required, as is vividly described in Ezekiel 40-48. During this future dispensation, the Two Commandments will again be applied by offering animal sacrifices in accordance with the instructions God will give.

---

[5] Scofield, C. (1909). *The Scofield Study Bible*. Pg. 5. Oxford University Press.

Additionally, the application of the Two Commandments can vary depending on the time period and culture you find yourself living in. For example, we are commanded to dress modestly in a way that does not flaunt our wealth (1 Timothy 2:9-10 and 1 Peter 3:3-4). However, the definition of economically modest or immodest clothing greatly varies depending on time period and culture. Oftentimes what is considered economically modest today in this culture would have been considered highly immodest when the New Testament was written. In ancient Roman culture, for instance, wearing purple clothing (which was very expensive to manufacture and typically worn only by royalty or nobility) would have been highly immodest; today, however, there is nothing special at all about purple clothing. Two thousand years ago, a Christian who wore purple clothing would have been breaking the Two Commandments; but, today, an American who wears purple clothing is not being disobedient to the Two Commandments.

APPLICATION TO CIVIL LAWS

Although there may be other factors which influence how the Two Commandments are applied, the previous paragraphs have laid a foundation sufficient for this study. With this out of the way, the application of the Law of God to human rights and civil laws can now be examined. As mentioned previously, according to Romans 13, governments are given authority by God to bring wrath upon those who do evil. To accomplish this, a nation must have laws that define good and evil behavior, establish basic human rights, and prescribe appropriate rewards for those who do good and punishments for those who do evil. The Law of God, which is the Two Commandments, must be the bedrock that determines these things.

When magistrates seek guidance on how to create just laws in their nations, including the establishment of human rights, the whole Word of God must be consulted. However, the laws found in the Old Testament will be of particular usefulness. Although the New Testament does have some insight for lawmakers, the main emphasis of these teachings is on the individual, the family, and the church. The Old Testament, on the other hand, places a larger emphasis on the nation of Israel and its civil laws and history, which should be of great interest to rulers and legislators. When considering whether or not a certain behavior should be illegal in his nation, a magistrate should ask a series of questions like the following:

Does this behavior violate the Two Commandments, to love God and love your neighbor?

If so, is this behavior condemned in the Bible?

What is the punishment for it?

Some sins, like pride, malice, jealousy, rejection of Christ, or the refusal of a believer to be baptized or attend church, for instance, are only punished by God (or, in some cases, the Church) and the Bible never instructs government officials to punish these offenses. If the Bible does describe a behavior as sinful and provides for a punishment to be administered by a national government, the lawmaker must also ask if this behavior is only wrong for people groups who are in a specific covenant relationship with God. For instance, if you are a politician in Denmark, Israelite sabbath laws are not applicable to you or your nation.

These same types of questions should be asked when a lawmaker is considering how to protect human rights in his nation.

To obey the command to love our neighbors, what human rights should we enshrine in our national laws?

Are there specific human rights which are protected in the Law of God or the teachings and examples found elsewhere in the Word of God? If so, we must acknowledge these rights in our laws.

Are there any human rights which, although not explicitly mentioned in the Bible, are in keeping with the totality of the teachings of the Word of God and show love to our neighbors in this present dispensation and culture? If there are, we should also protect these rights in our laws, since the command to love our neighbors as ourselves requires us to do so.

PERSONAL APPLICATION OF THE LAW

Before we move on to the next chapter where we will begin looking at specific human rights protected by God's Law, it is important for us to briefly look at how the Law should be applied in our daily lives and how this differs from the way it should be applied in lawmaking. Unfortunately, when it comes to the Law, many Christians confuse the role they play with the role of the state. For instance, a Christian who correctly understands that evildoers have made themselves the enemies of God and that the state should bring wrath on them may be tempted to treat evildoers in a manner that is rude, dehumanizing, merciless, and sometimes outright hostile. Worse yet, he may try to do the job of the state and enforce the penalty for perceived crimes himself.

Christians must remember that the Law of God is applied very differently in their daily lives compared to the role of the state when it comes to interactions with evildoers. If you are a Christian lawmaker, you should be God's minister of wrath against the wicked by writing just laws, and in so doing you love your neighbors in your nation; but, when you interact with an evildoer in your daily life, you should be kind, gentle, respectful, and wise in your interactions with them. You should love them by genuinely seeking their repentance and desiring to do good to them (1 Corinthians 10:24 and Galatians 6:10).

While the Old Testament is especially helpful for lawmakers and voters who desire to make laws that are in accordance with the Law of God, the New Testament is more applicable for learning how to apply the Law in your daily life. In the early church, very few Christians were in the government. Thus, the New Testament does not contain as much practical wisdom for Christian lawmakers who are seeking to apply the Law of God as the Old Testament does. However, because the New Testament was written when the New Covenant was inaugurated and the Holy Spirit began to write the Law of God on the hearts of believers, it is overflowing with practical wisdom for how to love God and love our neighbors in every area of daily life.

In the New Testament, we are told in Romans 12:21 to "not be overcome by evil, but [to] overcome evil with good." In Matthew 5:44-45, we are instructed,

> ...Love your enemies and pray for those who persecute you, so that you may be sons of your Father who is in heaven; for He causes His sun to rise on the evil and the good, and sends rain on the righteous and the unrighteous.

We are admonished in 1 Peter 3:8-9 to "be harmonious, sympathetic, brotherly, kindhearted, and humble in spirit; not returning evil for evil or insult for insult, but giving a blessing instead." In 1 Thessalonians 5:15, we are commanded, "See that no one repays another with evil for evil, but always seek after that which is good for one another and for all people." In 1 Corinthians 10:24, we are instructed, "Let no one seek his own good, but that of his neighbor." And, we are even given a beautiful picture of what love itself should look like in our daily lives in 1 Corinthians 13:4-7, which says:

> Love is patient, love is kind and is not jealous; love does not brag and is not arrogant, does not act unbecomingly; it does not seek its own, is not

> provoked, does not take into account a wrong suffered, does not rejoice in unrighteousness, but rejoices with the truth; bears all things, believes all things, hopes all things, endures all things.

After reading just this small sampling of the wisdom that the New Testament has to offer, no one should come away believing it is okay to dehumanize the wicked, treat them as if they were refuse, or take vengeance into our own hands. If God loves His enemies (Matthew 5:44-45) so much that He died for each and every one of them (1 John 2:2), shouldn't you love them too? After all, He died for you, even while you were sinner just like them (Romans 5:8 and Titus 3:3-7). After you have been forgiven of your great debts, will you act mercilessly to other sinners and treat them as if they are not even humans? Even sinners are made in the image of God and are loved by Him; accordingly, they deserve to be treated with love by you as well.

To conclude this chapter, I will share some of John Calvin's very moving thoughts on this topic, from his book *On the Christian Life*:

...We are not to pay attention to what people deserve in themselves but to reflect on the image of God in all people, to which we owe both respect and love. [...] Thus, no matter who you encounter who needs your help, you have no grounds for refusing to provide it. Say it is a stranger; but the Lord stamped that person with a mark that should be familiar to you, due to the fact that he forbids you to scorn your own flesh (Isaiah 58:7). Say they are repulsive and worthless; but the Lord points out that this is someone to whom he has granted the beauty of his image. Say you are not indebted to any service they have done for you; but God has, in a way, presented them as a substitute for himself so that in them you may recognize the many tremendous benefits with which God has obligated you to himself. Say that they are unworthy of even your least effort on their behalf; but the image of God, which commends them to you, is worthy of your handing over yourself and all you have. Even if they have deserved nothing good from you, and not only that, but have provoked you with insults and wrongdoing—not even this is just cause for you to stop embracing them in love and performing the duties of love toward them (Matthew 6:14[-15]; 18:35; Luke 17:3[-4]). You will say, "They deserve something far different from me." But what does the Lord deserve? When he directs you to forgive someone for whatever sins were committed against you, he clearly intends for those sins to be imputed to himself. This is really the only way to accomplish what is not only difficult but utterly contrary to human nature: to love those who hate us, to repay their acts of malice with good, and to reply to curses with blessings (Matthew 5:44). We must only remember that we should not reflect on people's malice but consider the image of God in them, which covers over and erases their offenses and which, by that image's beauty and dignity, draws us to love and embrace them."[6]

[6] Calvin, J. (2024). *On the Christian Life* (R.A. Blacketer, Trans.). Crossway. (Original work published 1550).

CHAPTER II

EQUAL RIGHTS FOR WOMEN, SINGLES, AND THE POOR

Withholding political and economic rights from women, singles, and those who don't own property is a prominent feature of modern and ancient pagan nations. Recently it has also received growing support in non-Christian right-wing political circles, as well as with wolves in the church. Not long ago, Joel Webbon, Christian political influencer and Pastor of Covenant Bible Church in Georgetown, Texas, had this to say about voting rights:

> If we ever got to the point where it was on the docket and it was something, ironically, that America was voting for—voting to take away the vote of women—me and my wife would both vote on principle, with conviction to take away her vote. [...] I believe in representative government at every single level all the way down to the

household. It doesn't go down to the individual; it stops at the household. […] The smallest building block of a nation's civic covenant is a family and not an individual. I actually think that, on principle, it's wrong for there to be more than a household vote.

[...] We currently live in a wicked time with wicked rulers who are dominated by feminism and hate men. […] What we're doing is having to get creative with the wicked landscape and [my wife is] ensuring that I have my full authority as a citizen. What the wicked rulers wanted to do is they want to strip away half of a man's authority and what [she's] doing is [she's] conceding it back to me by voting in line with the decision that I make for our family.

We think we should repeal the 19th [Amendment, which grants the right to vote to women in the United States] because we love God and because we love women. But beyond that, it's really more than just repealing the 19th. Universal suffrage is not God's design, so there's a lot of men

> who shouldn't be voting either. […] You need to be a head of household. […] You need to have a stake in the country as it presently lies, but also a stake in the future. That's why marriage is important because it indicates child-bearing, these kinds of things, future generations. A stake in the country also in terms of ownership; land owning males… It's not just women can't vote because they're too dumb to vote. That's not the position. […] Leaders should vote and God has given it to men to be leaders, and certain men have abdicated that leadership and therefore they should not have the right to vote either.[7]

There are a lot of statements to unpack here which are directly contradicted by the Law of God and the examples set by the saints of the Bible. The most glaringly obvious problem that must be pointed out first is that, if a plan like Webbon's was implemented, Jesus could not have voted. Jesus never married, had no

---

[7] Mantyla, K. (2024, November 1). 'Universal Suffrage Is Not God's Design': Christian Nationalist Joel Webbon Wants To Drastically Limit Voting Rights. People for the American Way. https://www.peoplefor.org/rightwingwatch/universal-suffrage-not-gods-design-christian-nationalist-joel-webbon-wants

children, and, as an itinerant preacher, was poor and had no land (Luke 9:58). If the King of Kings and Lord of Lords (1 Timothy 6:15 and Revelation 19:16) himself would not have been able to vote in someone's utopia, that person may want to pause and consider whether he actually thinks he is more fit to vote and govern than Jesus was during his earthly ministry.

In addition to Jesus, there are many other Biblical examples which challenge the notion that women, singles, and the poor can't be involved in politics by exercising their right to vote. Before getting to those examples, I will tear down Webbon's troublesome arguments and build up a Biblical case for giving all members of the nation a right to vote.

THE MOST FOUNDATIONAL FORM OF GOVERNMENT

First, let's look at the following claim: "The smallest building block of a nation's civic covenant is a family and not an individual. [...] On principle, it's wrong for there to be more than a household vote." This is completely false. Self-government is the most foundational form of government; without self-government, family government and civic government will both fail. If a man fails to govern himself and becomes a drunkard, he will not be a good husband, voter, or Congressman. Thus, since "the smallest building block of a nation's civic covenant" is the individual, using this logic it's wrong for there to be more than an individual vote. Arguing that a collective of people (e.g., the family) is the foundation of society instead of the individual reeks of socialistic collectivism.

A Stake in the Country

Second, the idea that "you need to have a stake in the country as it presently lies, but also a stake in the future" is fundamentally flawed and self-defeating. If the right to vote and be involved politically is dependent on how much of a relative "stake" someone has in the future of the nation, this could prove to be a good argument for the implementation of a legitimate aristocracy or oligarchy. After all, in this proposed system, women, poor apartment-dwellers who don't own land, and single people have been determined to not have "enough" of a stake in the future of the nation, and therefore don't deserve as much of a vote as one who may have a "greater stake." But from there, it's a small step to stripping away the political rights from the vast majority of Christian fathers who own land (even from Webbon who, for the sake of illustration, I will assume is a Christian father who owns land).

The owner of a major corporation owns thousands of properties, employs tens of thousands of employees, has millions of customers, and oversees billions of dollars worth of capital and investments. He has a much greater stake in the future of the nation than an insignificant property owner in Texas. Why does Webbon's vote get to "cancel out" the vote of an infinitely more important corporation owner? It would be totally absurd for this to happen, using the logic expressed in Webbon's statement.

To be logically consistent, relatively unimportant men like Pastor Webbon should not be allowed to vote or govern; that right should be reserved for those who have a *greater* stake in the future of the nation, like the owners of the ten most powerful corporations in the nation. This would result in an oligarchy. Alternatively, Webbon could still get one vote; but, the owner of the major corporation should get 800,000 votes, so that everything is fair, logically consistent, and Webbon doesn't get to cancel out the vote of someone who has much more of a stake in the country than he does. But, Webbon could lose even his meaningless single vote if he lost his job and the bank foreclosed on his house, or if he lost a lawsuit and had to sell his property to pay up. Since he would no longer be a property owner, he would lose all of his political rights. What a great system!

If you think I am being hyperbolic when I suggest that some of these men want an aristocracy, Webbon preached the following from the pulpit:

> It is actually a benefit when there is an aristocracy, whether formally or informally, meaning when there is a class of citizens that is a subset of the population as a whole that have been groomed and trained rigorously in virtue, in intellect, in philosophy, and most importantly the Scriptures and that they would be appointed to lead, and the

> peanut gallery wouldn't. But our "sacred democracy!" You know why Democrats love democracy so much? Because only when you have universal suffrage do you get a Democrat elected. It is only when you get the lowest IQ population, the poorest population, the highest statistically criminalized population, and give them an equal vote with "Heritage Americans" who have been here for four-hundred years who work hard, who pay the bulk of the taxes, and who are outstanding citizens who have not broken the law—It is only when you make everyone else an equal voter to them that you get someone like Ilhan Omar in a political office.[8]

As a side note, which demographic of the population is it that certain evil men constantly point out is the lowest IQ, poorest, and highest statistically-criminalized? Let the reader analyze Webbon's statement here and form his own conclusions

---

[8] Right Response Ministries. (2025, March 11). *"Inferiors & Superiors"* [Video]. YouTube. https://www.youtube.com/watch?v=4Tn2aRfRPWk&t=599s

about which demographic of the population he is advocating to deny equal voting rights to.

Webbon's comments here are almost laughably absurd. The Democrats got elected to public office for nearly a hundred years by men before women were given the right to vote with universal suffrage. Also, the vast majority of voters in Vermont would likely meet whatever Webbon's definition of a "Heritage American" is. It is one of the Whitest states in the country, with likely far more residents who can trace their ancestry back to colonial America than residents of most other states and, presumably, it has a very small amount of whatever demographic Webbon calls, "the lowest IQ, poorest, and highest statistically-criminalized." Yet, Vermont is also one of the most Democratic states in the nation.

It should be obvious that such a system, which denies political rights to the poor and effectively gives representation proportionally based on the amount of wealth someone has (even though it claims to be a system based on someone's "stake in the future of the nation"), is a horrible system of governance. Proverbs 29:7 states, "The righteous is concerned for the *rights* [emphasis added] of the poor, the wicked does not understand such concern."

Regarding these wicked men who seek to strip away equal rights from the poor, Proverbs 14:31 says, "He who oppresses the poor taunts his Maker, but he who is gracious to the needy honors Him." And, for those who desire to become patriarchs and aristocrats by taking away the rights of the poor, Proverbs 21:13 is an important warning: "He who shuts his ear to the cry of the poor will also cry himself and not be answered."

PARTIALITY AGAINST THE POOR

The last major point of disagreement that I have with Webbon's position is that "universal suffrage is not God's design," and here I will also start building my case for the fact that universal suffrage is indeed the preferred method of governance given by the Bible for Christian nations. The most important principle in support of this is the requirement under the Law of God for impartiality. James 2:9 states, "But if you show partiality, you are committing sin and are convicted by the law as transgressors." The specific way that this sin was being committed when James wrote his letter, in context (James 2:1-9), was against poor people:

> My brethren, do not hold your faith in our glorious Lord Jesus Christ with an attitude of personal favoritism. For if a man comes into your assembly with a gold ring and dressed in fine clothes, and there also comes in a poor man in dirty clothes, and you pay special attention to the one who is wearing the fine clothes, and say, "You sit here in a good place," and you say to the poor man, "You stand over there, or sit down by my footstool," have you not made distinctions among yourselves, and become judges with evil motives? Listen, my beloved brethren: did not God choose the poor of this world to be rich in faith and heirs of the kingdom which He promised to those who love Him? But you have dishonored the poor man. Is it not the rich who oppress you and personally drag you into court? Do they not blaspheme the fair name by which you have been called?

> If, however, you are fulfilling the royal law according to the Scripture, "You shall love your neighbor as yourself," you are doing well. But if you show partiality, you are committing sin and are convicted by the law as transgressors.

James would have a bone to pick with so-called "Christians" who advocate for taking away political rights from poor, apartment dwellers in the "peanut gallery" and giving them to richer land-owners. According to James, the poor are more likely to be rich in faith and heirs of the kingdom of God, thus making them much more fit to vote and govern in a Christian nation than the rich, who are more likely to be oppressors, those who sue Christians, and blasphemers of Christ. Thus, if wealth is going to be a factor in who gets a vote in a Christian nation (it should not be), votes should be taken away from rich, land-owning wannabe patriarchs, who are more likely to be oppressors and blasphemers of Christ, and only poor, apartment dwellers and renters, who are more likely to be rich in faith, should be allowed to vote.

PARTIALITY AGAINST WOMEN

Some patriarchalists are very transparent about their partiality against women. In a sermon that Joel Webbon preached from the pulpit, Webbon clarified that the reason he does not like female politicians is not primarily because of their policy decisions; rather, he dislikes them specifically because of their gender:

> When you say, "Well, I don't think that um… Well I disagree with uh… Pam Bondi, because I think she's hiding the Epstein files." And, I'd be like, "Yeah, but also I don't like Pam Bondi because she is a woman… and she shouldn't be in public. Not in politics." You know, like the meme that's like, "You and I are not the same. You don't like her for this reason. I don't like…" It's like, "Oh I don't like Pam Bondi because of her positions." And I'm like, "I don't like Pam Bondi because she needs to be at home."[9]

---

[9] Right Wing Watch. (2025, July 15). *Misogynistic Christian nationalist pastor Joel Webbon explains that he doesn't oppose Attorney General Pam Bondi because she's hiding the Epstein…* [Post with video from a sermon Joel Webbon preached]. X. https://x.com/RightWingWatch/status/1945147400923886002

The condemnation against partiality in the Bible not only includes partiality against poor people, but also applies to partiality against women. It is morally abominable for anyone to deny equal rights to others because he doesn't like their gender. All such partiality is strongly condemned by God's Law.

One of the things that makes the Law of God beautiful compared to the vulgar rules for society proposed by patriarchal pagan religions is that women are always equal to men when it comes to rights in court, politics, and employment. There are no rules which say that a woman's word is worth half as much as a man's; that it is fine for a husband to beat his wife; that a woman can only inherit half as much as a man; that a woman can't get a job outside the home; or that she can't vote or hold political office. When it comes to matters of civil law, politics, and labor, women are truly equal to men and God's Word does not prohibit them from doing anything a man can do.

One of the best examples in the Bible which illustrates this fact is the person of Deborah, who can be read about in Judges 4 and 5. She was a prophetess who was also the chief judge over the whole nation of Israel (Judges 4:4). Deborah was married, but when it came to leading the nation, she was at the top. She out-ranked all men. Not only that, but she accompanied and helped lead the Israelite army which went out to fight the Canaanite invaders (Judges 4:9-10, 14). God blessed Deborah and gave her victory, even causing the Canaanite general Sisera to be humiliatingly killed by a woman (Judges 4:21), which Deborah had prophesied would happen (Judges 4:9).

Deborah is one of the only judges mentioned in the Bible who was spotless in her service as a judge. Unlike the other male judges, there is no record of Deborah vowing to sacrifice one of her own daughters (Judges 11:30-40), bowing down to idols (Judges 8:27), or sleeping with prostitutes (Judges 16:1). She was a perfect judge and she was a woman.

This is one of the most perplexing Biblical stories for those who are sinfully partial against the female sex, believing that males are superior to women in matters of politics and economics. If Deborah could be one of the best national political leaders in the history of Israel (out-ranking all men) and even help lead men in combat, Biblically-speaking, what is off limits for women politically or career-wise? If a married woman can be the Commander in Chief of a nation and its military, why can't she vote for who the Commander in Chief should be? Why can't she be a senator, the CEO of a corporation, a police chief, or a manager at a Chick-Fil-A?

The primary way patriarchalists try to reject the idea that Deborah is an example for women today is to argue that the men in Deborah's day refused to "step up," so God appointed Deborah to humiliate the men. But, this objection falls flat on its face because, even if this statement was true, who is to say that God is not doing the same thing today? Patriarchalists are fond of complaining about today's multitudes of "weak" and "effeminate" men after all. Isn't it possible that God is raising up some Deborahs today to humiliate these multitudes of "weak" and "effeminate" men? If these patriarchalists lived during Deborah's day, they would likely have told her to "stay home" and ignore God's call on her life, like they do with God's daughters today. Ultimately, this is not a serious objection, since there is essentially no possible world today where patriarchalists would be okay with God raising up another Deborah.

Those who use man-invented traditions to take away the rights of women and subjugate them under the rule of men in politics and the labor force are the same as those described by Jesus in Mark 7:8, where He says, "Neglecting the commandment of God, you hold to the tradition of men." They don't like women, are partial against them, and don't want to live in any world where women can vote, hold political office, have a job outside the home, or even be seen in public.

Women Rule Over Them

There are four primary passages in Scripture which a patriarchalist may use to support his view that women should not be allowed to participate in politics or work outside the home. The first is Isaiah 3:12, which says, "O My people! Their oppressors are children, and women rule over them. O My people! Those who guide you lead you astray and confuse the direction of your paths."

In context, this verse occurs in a passage which is describing God's judgements on rebellious Israel. The point of this verse is not that women are inherently bad rulers or that God only gives female rulers as a part of a judgement against a nation which is designed to further destroy the nation. If so, it would be inconsistent with the story of Deborah. Rather, this verse states that God gave ancient Israel (in Isaiah's day) female rulers who were bad. They were not bad because they were female, they were bad rulers because they were bad people.

To hit this point home, Isaiah 3:6 says, "When a man lays hold of his brother in his father's house, saying, 'You have a cloak, you shall be our ruler, and these ruins will be under your charge.'" If the patriarchalist used the same hermeneutic to interpret this passage as he does for verse 12, this verse would be saying that God punishes a nation by giving them male voters (a "*man*" who lays hold of his brother and says, "You have a cloak, *you shall be our ruler*") and that all males are inherently stupid and choose terrible leaders. That would be an incredibly moronic way to interpret this verse, but it would be logically consistent for the patriarchalist. Without a doubt, a much better way to interpret this verse is to say that God punished ancient Israel by giving the nation stupid men who made foolish decisions in who they chose as their leaders. It had nothing to do with these individuals being male. These particular stupid people who God used in this particular situation in ancient Israel just happened to be male.

There is another problem to a universal application of this verse ripped out of its Israel-specific context. If it was true that female rulers are always a judgment from God on a nation designed to bring about their ruin, why on earth have there been so many nations throughout history which have flourished under female rulers? England experienced its "golden age" under the rule of Queen Elizabeth I. Russia prospered during the reign of Queen Catherine the Great. The United Kingdom experienced many successes while Margaret Thatcher was Prime Minister. Taiwan underwent many economic and political triumphs while Tsai Ing-wen was President. Empress Cixi of China modernized her nation and made significant reforms which were good for her people. There are many examples of female rulers like this, proving that the correct interpretation of this verse is not universal, but was only specific to Israel in Isaiah's day.

WORKERS AT HOME

Pharisaical patriarchalists not only teach that women should not be allowed to hold positions in public office; like ancient and modern pagans, they also teach that women should not be allowed to be visible in public at all. Pastor Joel Webbon made the following claim on his show:

> In a nutshell, in general, I don't want to see women in the public sphere. You mean, they shouldn't hold political office? Correct. You mean, you don't want to see them podcasting? Correct. But, what about in the marketplace, you know, with nine-to-five careers? No, not that either. I don't want to see women holding positions in the public square… I don't."[10]

---

[10] Mantyla, K. (2025, March 5). Joel Webbon Does Not Want To See Women In The Public Sphere. People for the American Way. [Video]. https://www.peoplefor.org/rightwingwatch/joel-webbon-does-not-want-see-women-public-sphere

It is important to note that Webbon is being highly hypocritical here, since he has been on multiple women's podcasts, even in the year prior to making this statement.[11,12]

Pastor and musician Brian Sauvé also entered the fray by saying,

> When a woman fighter pilot crashes her plane, she has made two errors: Being in the plane in the first place and then crashing it. When a male fighter pilot crashes his plane, he has made one mistake: Crashing it. Women in principle are not fitted [sic] for civil rule.[13]

A passage that is sometimes cited by these patriarchalists to justify why women can't have jobs outside the home is Titus 2:3-5, which says,

> Older women likewise are to be reverent in their behavior, not malicious gossips nor enslaved to

---

[11] Guest appearances. (n.d.). Right Response Ministries. https://rightresponseministries.com/shows/guest-appearances/

[12] Right Response Ministries. (2024, April 16). *Pearl Davis Interviews Pastor Joel Webbon | Biblical Patriarchy & Christian Nationalism* [Video]. YouTube. https://www.youtube.com/watch?v=cSwkTO_m8nY

[13] Sauvé, B. (2025, March 6). *When a woman fighter pilot crashes her plane, she has made two errors: Being in the plane in the first...* [Post]. X. https://x.com/Brian_Sauve/status/1897723973070471318

> much wine, teaching what is good, so that they may encourage the young women to love their husbands, to love their children, to be sensible, pure, workers at home, kind, being subject to their own husbands, so that the word of God will not be dishonored.

However, this verse does not say that being a "worker at home" is a responsibility exclusive to women any more than it is saying that "loving their children" is an exclusively feminine task. Both working at home and loving children are the responsibility of mothers *and* fathers.

In Ephesians 6:4, when Paul says, "Fathers, do not provoke your children to anger," there is no hidden implication that it is okay for a mother to provoke her children to anger, because not provoking children is exclusively the responsibility of the father. Rather, Paul knew that the fathers in that particular church needed to be exhorted not to provoke their children to wrath (presumably, the women did not have this problem). Similarly, the younger women in Titus' sphere of influence needed to be exhorted not to neglect their household duties (presumably, the men did not have this problem). Logic and the context of this verse do not allow it to be over-extended in its reach to say that women cannot work outside the house.

To conclusively prove this verse does not mean what the patriarchalist thinks it does, Proverbs 31 (verses 13, 14, and 16) indicates that a woman can and should leave the house if needed for work and can even start her own business enterprise:

> She looks for wool and flax and works with her hands in delight. She is like merchant ships; she brings her food from afar. [...] She considers a field and buys it; from her earnings she plants a vineyard.

Without a doubt, it is Biblically permissible and even required for women to be allowed to enter the public square and be seen. If this was forbidden, then it would not be possible for women to obey Proverbs 31.

Was Deborah sinning when she judged the nation of Israel publicly? How about when she led Israelite troops in battle? Was it wrong for Huldah, a married prophetess, to deliver messages from God to the king (2

Kings 22:14-20)? If a woman can be the leader of a nation, command troops in battle, and deliver prophetic messages from God to the king, what grounds do proud, insecure, whiny men have to tell her that she can't fly an airplane, drive a car, have a podcast, or work a nine-to-five job? Is it wrong for Christian women to have jobs as midwives (Exodus 1:15-20), managers for government officials (Luke 8:3), tentmakers (Acts 18:2-3), or merchants of expensive purple fabrics (Acts 16:14)? These jobs were held by faithful saints who used the income that they gained to help support their families and, in some cases, used what they earned to support the ministry of Jesus (Luke 8:2-3) and the early church (1 Corinthians 16:19).

Proud, pharisaical wolves who condemn these New Testament saints and who afflict and dishonor God's precious daughters today should remember that these women have a mighty Father who cares about them and who is coming soon to deal with those who have afflicted and abused them and treated them like worthless property (2 Thessalonians 1:6-8).

NOT PERMITTED TO TEACH OR EXERCISE AUTHORITY

The next passage that patriarchalists attempt to rip out of context to indicate that women can never have authority over men is 1 Timothy 2:9-12, where Paul says,

> Likewise, I want women to adorn themselves with proper clothing, modestly and discreetly, not with braided hair and gold or pearls or costly garments, but rather by means of good works, as is proper for women making a claim to godliness. A woman must quietly receive instruction with entire submissiveness. But I do not allow a woman to teach or exercise authority over a man, but to remain quiet.

Again, in this passage, Paul is giving exhortation that the women in Timothy's sphere of influence specifically needed to hear (i.e., be economically modest, receive instruction, and be submissive), although these commands are not exclusively for women (for instance, the Bible specifically says that men must be submissive as well, according to Ephesians 5:21 and 1 Peter 5:5). When

Paul says that he does “not allow a woman to teach or exercise authority over a man, but to receive instruction with entire submissiveness” this is a gender specific command. However, this command clearly is only in regards to gender roles in the church and, even then, there are many exceptions to this. Even in church, women can still serve as deacons, according to 1 Timothy 3:11 and can pray and prophesy, according to 1 Corinthians 11:5.

But it cannot be a general command meaning that women can never have authority over men outside the church. If that was the case, a mother could not teach or have authority over her male children (Ephesians 6:1 and Colossians 3:20 indicate that both parents have authority over all of their children) and could not be the judge of a nation and a military commander (Deborah was both). Paul does not contradict himself or any other writing in the Holy Scriptures. He obviously intended for this command to only be applied in church as it relates to pastoral positions. So, it is completely inappropriate to use this verse to mean something that Paul never intended for it to mean.

Man's Clothing

Deuteronomy 22:5 is used by some patriarchalists to say that women aren't allowed to have certain types of "manly" jobs, such as serving in the military or law enforcement:

> A woman shall not wear man's clothing, nor shall a man put on a woman's clothing; for whoever does these things is an abomination to the LORD your God.

It should be obvious to any person who reads this verse without a preconceived agenda that this command is in regards to clothing, not jobs, and the specific sin that it is dealing with is transvestism, which was commonly practiced in pagan temple orgies. John MacArthur wrote the following about this verse:

> Found only here in the Pentateuch, this statute prohibited a man from wearing any item of feminine clothing or ornamentation, or a woman from wearing any item of masculine clothing or ornamentation. The same word translated 'abomination' was used to describe God's view of

> homosexuality (Lv 18:22, 20:13). This instance specifically out-lawed transvestism. The creation order distinctions between male and female were to be maintained without exception.[14]

If this verse is not simply referring to sexually-perverted transvestism, but is referring to the type of clothing that men and women wear for work, many issues arise. In American society, for instance, men and women both wear pants, button-up shirts, and carry guns. How on earth is a female police officer, who wears pants, a button-up shirt, and carries a gun (which is normal for her gender), violating this command?

If a patriarchalist insists that it is not normal for women to wear pants and that only skirts are feminine, then a female police officer could hypothetically just wear a skirt and she would not be violating this command (and the patriarchalist would have to be okay with that, if he actually cared about what he claimed to care about). Additionally, this hermeneutic works both ways: I could argue that nursing scrubs are feminine clothing.

---

[14] MacArthur, J. (2020). *The MacArthur Study Bible*. Pg. 233. Thomas Nelson, a division of HarperCollins Christian Publishing, Inc.

According to the logic of a patriarchalist who interprets this verse, men can never be nurses. This would prove to be highly problematic for society, since patriarchalists also believe that women can't work outside the home, meaning that neither men nor women could be nurses.

More sophisticated patriarchalists will point out that the Hebrew word for men's "clothing" used in Deuteronomy 22:5, "*keli*," is *sometimes* translated as "armor," "weapons," and "implements of violence," elsewhere in the Old Testament. Although this is true, the specific context of the passage at hand is the most important thing for determining how the word should be translated, especially in a language like Hebrew where words have many different meanings.

The word *keli* is very flexible in its meaning and is variously translated as "clothing," "gears," "baggage," "utensils," "vessels," "pottery," "yokes," "furnishings," "jars," and "articles," in addition to "armor," "weapons," and "implements of violence." Using the hermeneutic of the patriarchalist, it would make just as much sense to say that Deuteronomy 22:5 is commanding women not to use a man's pottery or his baggage.

But let's assume that the patriarchalist is right; all the Bible translations which refer to *keli* in Deuteronomy 22:5 as men's "clothing" are wrong, and the patriarchalists are among the only people who got it right—the proper interpretation should have been men's "armor," "weapons," or "implements of violence" all along. If that is the case, the first problem to arise is the following question: which types of armor, weapons, and implements of violence are considered to be uniquely men's and which, if any, are considered to be women's?

The patriarchalist would probably say that swords, shields, bows, suits of armor, knives, firearms, and modern body armor are uniquely considered to be men's. However, since that is the case, this means that their wives can never carry firearms or knives, or use modern body armor, *in any situation* (for self-defense, or otherwise), since to bear such items would make a woman appear to be like a man, in violation of Deuteronomy 22:5. Does the patriarchalist really want to establish the idea that it is immoral for their wives to carry handguns and defend themselves with them, because handguns are considered to be a man's weapon?

The patriarchalist may object, "But they will only be using handguns for self-defense or the defense of others! They're not going to be the aggressors." This would be a highly arbitrary response, given their interpretation of the passage (since, ostensibly, it has nothing to do with using weapons offensively or defensively, but is all about whether certain weapons are masculine or feminine). If women can use handguns for self-defense or the defense of others, that means women can be police officers, since that is exactly the reason police officers carry weapons. Even soldiers commonly make the argument that they are using their weapons merely to defend themselves and their nations.

Additionally, there is a "feminine weapon" problem with this strained interpretation of the verse. If certain weapons can (somehow) be masculine, it logically follows that certain weapons can (somehow) be feminine. If that is the case, weapons or implements of violence that would certainly be feminine are hammers and tent pegs. Why? Because Jael, a woman, used a hammer and a tent peg as a weapon to kill Sisera, an enemy invader (Judges 4:21). Also, Judges 9:53 describes a woman who used a stone as a weapon by dropping it on the head of a murderous military leader, Abimelech, resulting in his death.

If it is morally wrong for women to bear men's weapons because this is sinful transvestism, it would be consistent to say it is morally wrong for men to bear women's weapons, as this would make them appear to be like women and also be sinful transvestism. This means it would be morally wrong for men to use hammers or pick up stones. However, there are men in the Bible, like King David, who used stones, even as weapons (1 Samuel 17:40), and men like Moses and Israelite craftsmen who were commanded to use hammers (Exodus 25:31 and 39:3). The idea that certain weapons can be masculine or feminine results in obvious absurdities and contradictions.

As you can see, it is remarkable what depths patriarchalists must sink to in order to find scriptural justification for the sinful partiality they harbor against women. Like those in cults, they rip verses out of context and make clear verses unclear to justify their bizarre ideas. They are like those who pluck the question posed in 1 Corinthians 15:29, "If the dead are not raised at all, why then are they baptized for them?" from its context and use it to justify their strange doctrine of baptizing for the dead. This idea, like the notion that women can't be involved in politics, police, the military, or have jobs outside of the home, is clearly contradicted by the rest of the Bible. But if your evidence is only a handful of verses devoid of their context and you are not familiar with the rest of the Bible, the arguments for baptizing the dead and patriarchalism may sound very convincing to you.

THE UNDERESTIMATED WOMAN

The last argument made for not allowing women to serve in the military, police, or political positions is that women are not emotionally or physically capable of handling things that were only meant for big, tough, manly men, like making consequential decisions, being brave, doing things which are physically exerting, enduring pain, and seeing horrifying sights. "It is a well-known fact that women can't handle the sight of blood," says a foolish man with absolutely no knowledge of the female menstrual cycle. Once again, such a claim is directly contradicted by the Bible.

Did Deborah not make consequential decisions? Was she not brave? Was Jael not brave when she deceived an enemy commander, set him at ease, and quickly drove a tent stake through his head with a hammer? Do you think that this was not a horrifying sight? If that was not a horrifying thing to do and see, there is nothing too horrifying for women to do and see. Don't you think that this act required significant physical exertion? I don't think Jael was just lightly tapping on that tent peg with the hammer. What about the woman who dropped a stone on Abimelech's head? Don't you think that this required physical exertion? How about Mary, the mother of Jesus? Didn't she physically exert herself and endure pain when she gave birth to Jesus? It is preposterous that many men think women aren't as capable of enduring physical exertion or pain as well as them, because such sentiments display a stunning lack of awareness of what the childbirthing process is like.

EQUAL RIGHTS FOR SINGLE PEOPLE

In addition to protecting the political rights of women, God's Word also protects the political rights of singles. Stripping away political rights from singles because they are singles would make a nation guilty of the same sin described previously, the sin of partiality (James 2:9). Denying political representation to singles is not only against the Law of God, but it is imbecilic to say that Jeremiah, John the Baptist, and Paul, some of the greatest saints who ever lived, should be denied the ability to vote or hold political office. The position is also contradicted by the examples of these men, since all three were single and involved in politics to some degree. John the Baptist was imprisoned because he meddled in the political sphere by condemning Herod for violating the Law after he married his brother's wife (Mark 6:18). Was it wrong for John the Baptist to meddle in political affairs because he didn't have a "vested stake in the future of his nation" as a single person?

In Acts 24:24-25, Governor Felix summoned Paul to have a personal conversation with him and Paul preached “righteousness, self-control and the judgment to come” to Felix. Righteousness, self-control, and the judgment to come certainly had implications for Felix politically and for his work as a governor. Was it wrong for Paul to get involved in Felix’s political affairs, since Paul did “not have a vested interest in the future of his nation” as a single? How can it be permissible for a single Christian to advise a magistrate on the importance of making righteous decisions, but be forbidden from voting for the magistrate or becoming a magistrate himself?

Likewise, Jeremiah delivered prophetic messages and instructions to the King of Judah which had significant political ramifications (Jeremiah 37:7-10 and 38:14-26). Was it wrong for Jeremiah to get involved in the politics of Judah when he “didn’t have a vested political interest in the future of his nation” as a single? If Jeremiah can speak the words of God to a political leader just like any other Christian single with a Bible can, why should that saint be forbidden from putting the words of God into action by voting for righteousness or even becoming a political leader and making a righteous decree? Those who know their Bibles know that

Jeremiah, John the Baptist, and Paul all had "vested interests in the future of their nations" even though they were singles. Clearly, the Law and the examples found in the Bible indicate that singles should have their political rights protected in a Christian nation.

ALL THE PEOPLE

So what would voting look like in a Christian nation? I believe the Biblical model is universal suffrage. Over and over again in the Old Testament, whenever covenants are confirmed with the nation of Israel, they are confirmed by assemblies consisting of *everyone* in the nation, regardless of whether they were small or great or male or female. When God was confirming his covenants with the people of Israel, there truly was no partiality regarding who was allowed to assent or dissent to the ratification or reaffirmation of the covenant. The first account of this can be found in Exodus 24:3, where it says,

> Then Moses came and recounted to the people all the words of the LORD and all the ordinances;

> and *all the people* [emphasis added] answered with one voice and said, "All the words which the LORD has spoken we will do!"

The covenant was re-confirmed in Joshua 24:7, which states,

> Joshua said to *all the people* [emphasis added], "Behold, this stone shall be for a witness against us, for it has heard all the words of the LORD which He spoke to us; thus it shall be for a witness against you, so that you do not deny your God."

Lastly, in 2 Kings 23:1-3, when King Josiah discovered a lost book of the Law, he and the people of Judah made a covenant with the Lord to obey it:

> Then the king sent, and they gathered to him all the elders of Judah and of Jerusalem. The king went up to the house of the LORD and all the men of Judah and all the inhabitants of Jerusalem with him, and the priests and the prophets and *all the people, both small and great* [emphasis added]; and he read in their hearing all the words of the book of the covenant which was found in the house of the LORD. The king stood by the pillar

> and made a covenant before the LORD, to walk after the LORD, and to keep His commandments and His testimonies and His statutes with all his heart and all his soul, to carry out the words of this covenant that were written in this book. And *all the people* [emphasis added] entered into the covenant.

If all the people of a nation, including the small and great and male and female, can be present to assent or dissent to making a covenant with Almighty God, a matter of infinite importance, then why can't they vote on temporal political matters which, comparatively, are much less important? I believe that a Christian nation should follow this example and extend voting and political rights to every member of the nation without partiality. People should have this right for as long as they live and it should never be taken away, even if they are convicted of crimes.

Children and Criminals

There are two objections that I would anticipate to this. First, someone may ask, "What about children?

Wouldn't you be showing partiality against children by not allowing them to vote?" Since children do not understand the difference between right and wrong (Deuteronomy 1:39), which is essential for voting, I think there are Biblical grounds for not extending the right to vote to children. Alternatively, a Christian nation could give votes to children, but could require these votes to be stewarded by their caretakers (biological parents, adopted parents, or legal guardians) until they reach an age when they are able to understand the difference between right and wrong.

Second, someone may object to allowing those convicted of crimes to vote. It is important to remember that, in a nation which is obeying God's Law, those convicted of major crimes against the image of God (such as rape and murder) should not be allowed to live and will not be voting (Genesis 9:6 and Deuteronomy 22:25-27). In such a nation, there will not be men walking around freely in society who were justly convicted of the crime of raping a child and were released after serving two years in prison. They will be executed by the state and will not be voting in any elections.

For those convicted of minor offenses like property crimes, what could possibly be the reason for denying political rights to them for the rest of their lives, especially after they have made full restitution for their crimes and been restored to society? Such a punishment would not be appropriate or just in any sense. The ability to take away people's votes or right to participate in politics after they are convicted of crimes also creates a significant moral hazard, as it is a weighty motivation for those in power to falsely accuse and convict their political enemies of crimes.

A VOTE FOR CEASAR

In summary, the Law of God and the examples set by the saints in the Word of God make it abundantly clear that a Christian nation must extend full and equal political and labor force participation rights to women, singles, and poor people who don't own property. Partiality and denial of political rights for any group of people on account of their gender, marital status, fertility status, wealth, or poverty should never be the case in a nation that lives by the instructions of Christ.

Those who advocate for stripping away political rights from their neighbors and placing them in the hands of an aristocracy (which, conveniently, they will be a part of) should not forget that other power-hungry men will use the same arguments they are using to take away their political voice as well. The tendency of humanity is always to surrender its power to an increasingly smaller class of elites, reaching its culmination when one man alone has total power. Consolidating power in the hands of a patriarchy will not be the end of the consolidation of power. Men will cry out for a Caesar to save them, just like what happened to the ancient Roman patriarchalists. Like the Israelites begging for a king in Samuel 8:7, those who pursue this corrupting path have rejected God as their king.

CHAPTER III

EQUAL RIGHTS REGARDLESS OF RACE, ETHNICITY, OR STATUS AS A FOREIGNER

> "France to the French, England to the English, America to the Americans, and Germany to the Germans. We are resolved to prevent the settlement in our country of a strange people which was capable of snatching for itself all the leading positions in the land, and to oust it. [...] Above all, German culture, as its name alone shows, is German [...], and therefore its management and care will be entrusted to members of our own nation." - Unattributed

Many Christians who read through the Bible for the first time are surprised to learn that the Bible unambiguously protects the rights of foreigners, granting them the same legal protections as the native-born. Some of the passages which teach this include:

> The stranger who resides with you shall be to you as the native among you, and you shall love him as yourself, for you were aliens in the land of Egypt; I am the LORD your God. (Leviticus 19:34)
>
> There shall be one standard for you; it shall be for the stranger as well as the native, for I am the LORD your God. (Leviticus 24:22)
>
> You shall not oppress a stranger, since you yourselves know the feelings of a stranger, for you also were strangers in the land of Egypt. (Exodus 23:9)
>
> He [God] executes justice for the orphan and the widow, and shows His love for the alien by giving him food and clothing. So show your love for the alien, for you were aliens in the land of Egypt. (Deuteronomy 10:18-19)

If these passages from God's Law offend someone or make him squirm, he should pay close attention to what God's Word teaches on this subject. A true Christian must not ignore or be ashamed of the Word of God. In Luke 9:26, Jesus warns, "For whoever is ashamed of Me and *My words* [emphasis added], the Son of Man will be ashamed of him when He comes in His glory, and the glory of the Father and of the holy angels."

The Hebrew word *ger*, translated here as "stranger" or "alien" by the NASB 1995, is most commonly translated as "foreigner" by new translations (NIV, NLT, BSB, HCSB, CEV, NET, and others), but is also sometimes translated as "sojourner" by others. From its context and usage, it is clear that the word applies in its coverage to anyone residing in a nation who is not considered to be one of the people of the nation. This would certainly include someone who was born or grew up in a foreign nation, but would also likely apply to someone who is of a race or ethnicity which is considered to be foreign by the people of the nation. An example of this would be descendants of Black slaves who resided in America their whole lives but who were denied political rights under Jim Crow laws in many states due to their perceived status as strangers or sub-citizens. Regardless, however, the point of these commands is that the law must be equal for everyone in the nation, regardless of whether they are considered to be a foreigner or a native.

It bears repeating that James 2:9 admonishes, “But if you show partiality, you are committing sin and are convicted by the law as transgressors.” If there is one law for people who are considered “natives” of the nation and another law for those who are considered “foreigners” (especially if it results in them being oppressed), this is sinful partiality which is condemned by God’s Law. A Christian nation cannot have laws which (as written or as enforced) result in the deportation of people who are considered to be “foreigners” for criminal offenses when the same punishment is not given to those who are considered to be natives who commit the same offenses. Leviticus 24:22 states, “There shall be one standard for you; it shall be for the stranger as well as the native, for I am the LORD your God.” However a criminal offense is punished for the native, the same punishment must be given to the foreigner.

If someone does not like this, his problem is with the Law of God. How can someone read sections of God’s Law that he likes (for instance, passages which forbid murder, rape, or theft) and then have problems with other sections of God's Law that he does not like (e.g., passages which give equal rights to foreigners)? James 2:10 warns, "For whoever keeps the whole law and yet stumbles in one point, he has become guilty of all." Such individuals must be exhorted to not be simpletons, but to repent of their sinful beliefs and let the Law of God make them wise. As Psalm 19:7 says, "The law of the LORD is perfect, restoring the soul; the testimony of the LORD is sure, making wise the simple."

Does *Ger* Refer to a Temporary Resident?

Before continuing, I will address a couple of objections that have been presented by those who misinterpret the laws concerning foreigners so they can avoid obeying the laws as literally written and understood. First, some argue that the word *ger* is only used to describe temporary residents and sojourners; not foreigners who want to come to a nation, join the nation, and stay there forever. So a nation must treat foreigners equally and fairly for a few months or years at most, but once they have overstayed their welcome, then they can be treated unequally and unfairly.

Although it is true that the word "*ger*" can refer to temporary residents, it can also be used to describe foreigners who will reside in a land for an indefinitely long period of time. When Leviticus 19:34 says, "The stranger [*ger*] who resides with you shall be to you as the native among you, and you shall love him as yourself, for you were aliens [*ger*] in the land of Egypt," the word *ger* is used to describe both the foreigners who are supposed to be treated equally by the Israelites and the Israelites who were foreigners in Egypt. However, according to Exodus 12:40-41, the Israelites were foreigners in Egypt for four-hundred and thirty years.

So a foreigner and his descendants are considered to be like the Israelites and eligible for protection under Leviticus 19:34 (and other passages) for four-hundred and thirty years at the bare minimum (which would really try the patience of political reactionaries who want vengeance on the foreigners they hate *right now*, in their lifetimes). Even after that, there is no place in Scripture which suggests or implies that there is any point when a *ger* overstays his welcome and loses protections under Leviticus 19:34.

Ger vs. *Zar*

Second, some people try to make the opposite claim and will argue that *ger* refers to "good foreigners" who always assimilate into the nation they sojourn in and leave behind every aspect of their former nationality and ethnicity. This is in contrast with the Hebrew word *zar*, which they interpret to mean "bad foreigners," and are characterized by being foreigners who do not assimilate into the nation they are sojourning in; these foreigners are always portrayed in a negative light by the Bible.

To start with, it is important to note that *ger* and *zar* are not the only Hebrew words used to describe foreigners (*nachar* and *ben* are also used, often in a positive light). It is an oversimplification to try to divide all foreigners neatly into the categories of *ger* and *zar* for the purposes of making a political point. Although it is true that *zar* is usually used to describe certain foreigners in a negative light in the Old Testament, there is no place in the entire Bible that remotely alludes to or implies the idea that *ger* assimilate and *zar* do not. Those who make this claim are practicing eisegesis (reading things into the text that are not there). Exegesis (reading things out of the text), on the other hand, shows that the opposite is true.

As pointed out previously, *ger* is used to describe the Israelites in Egypt in Leviticus 19:34 and other texts. The Israelites did not assimilate into Egypt. *Ger* is also used by Abaraham to describe himself when he was in the midst of the Hittites (Genesis 23:4). Abraham never assimilated into the Hittites. So, the idea that the Law of God allows us to treat foreigners unequally and unfairly if they do not assimilate is false and wicked.

So why are *zar* portrayed in a bad light? It is because this word is used to describe specific foreigners who do specific bad things (oppressing the poor, acting violently, enticing others to commit adultery, etc.). It has nothing to do with an imagined failure to assimilate. Those who make this assertion are ignorant at best, and malevolently dishonest at worst.

DEPORTATION AS A PUNISHMENT

Others will attempt to argue that deportation is a punishment that is prescribed by the Law for some offenses. When asked for verses that support this, they will usually cite passages like the following:

> And any man from the house of Israel, or from the aliens who sojourn among them, who eats any blood, I will set My face against that person who eats blood and will cut him off from among his people. (Leviticus 17:10)
>
> For anyone of the house of Israel or of the immigrants who stay in Israel who separates himself from Me, sets up his idols in his heart, puts right before his face the stumbling block of his iniquity, and then comes to the prophet to inquire of Me for himself, I the LORD will be brought to answer him in My own person. I will set My face against that man and make him a sign and a proverb, and I will cut him off from among My people. So you will know that I am the LORD." (Ezekiel 14:7-8)

> But the person who does anything defiantly, whether he is native or an alien, that one is blaspheming the LORD; and that person shall be cut off from among his people. (Numbers 15:30)

First, it is important to point out that the punishment of being "cut off," whatever that is, is applied equally to the native-born as well as the foreigner. Whatever crime a foreigner is cut off for, the native must be as well, since there is one standard for the native and the foreigner (Leviticus 24:22). If a foreigner is deported for driving under the influence, the native must be as well. This does nothing to help the case of those who are partial against foreigners, since they usually only want to deport foreigners and not natives.

However, among Old Testament scholars, there is very little support for the notion that "cut off" refers to exile or deportation; the vast majority of scholars, commentators, and theologians believe that the phrase refers to death. A minority argue that the phrase refers to being cut off from the Israelite religious community (today, in the church age, this would be the equivalent of excommunication from the church). But the idea that this is referring to exile or deportation is novel and held to by very few in scholarly circles.

The context of these passages strongly suggests that "cut off" is referring to death as a punishment that is carried out by God Himself or as excommunication from the religious community. According to Numbers 15:30, the person who "does anything" (any sin) "defiantly" must be cut off. If this was referring to deportation, the state would be required to deport anyone (citizen or non-citizen) for *any* sin or violation of God's Law that was conducted "defiantly," regardless of "whether he is native or an alien." If you steal a candy bar defiantly, you get deported. If you trespass on private property defiantly, you get deported. If you defiantly write a hot check, you get deported. This is obviously absurd.

A much better understanding of this phrase is that we should expect God to put to death any person who arrogantly chooses to sin as an act of true defiance against Him and His Law. Alternatively, another good explanation would be to say that the religious community in Israel (or, today, the church) should excommunicate any person who defiantly continues to sin after being warned and rebuked by his brothers and the congregation multiple times (Matthew 18:15-17). Either of these explanations makes more sense than trying to say that "cut off" refers to deportation, which is one of the reasons why almost all scholars reject this notion.

NO DISTINCTION UNDER THE LAW

After all of his eisegetical objections have been answered, the last thing that someone who doesn't want to obey Leviticus 19:34 can say is, "Well, you seem to think that Leviticus 19:34 applies to any foreigner who is in your nation regardless of how he got there." This isn't a good argument, partly because it is true. Leviticus 19:34 does not make any distinctions regarding how foreigners got in the nation when it comes to treating them equally, so neither do I. It is wrong to add extra-Biblical loopholes to the Law in an attempt to violate it. The Pharisees in Jesus' day did this, and it is something that people still do today.

Usually, those opposed to obeying Leviticus 19:34 as it is naturally interpreted are also opposed to homosexuality, which is condemned in passages like Leviticus 18:22, where it says, "You shall not lie with a male as one lies with a female; it is an abomination." These people would vehemently disagree with liberal theologians who nullify verses like Leviticus 18:22 by arguing that all verses prohibiting homosexuality in the Bible were actually referring to abusive pagan temple practices and, therefore, such practices are fine today as long as they are not abusive. The irony is that someone does exactly the same thing if he opposes immigration and adds stipulations to verses like Leviticus 19:34 which effectively nullify the commands given in the verse.

Laws Not Based in Morality

Not only should a Christian nation treat foreigners equally, but it should not prohibit immigration. As mentioned previously, God's purpose for civil government is outlined clearly in Romans 13: commending those who do good, bringing wrath on those who do evil, and securing revenue to accomplish this purpose. Any law which falls outside of these categories exceeds God's defined role for civil governments and is null and void. Governments must not make laws which forbid, restrict, discourage, or otherwise inhibit people from doing things which are morally lawful.

China's former "one-child" policy, which prohibited parents from having more than one child, is a perfect example of this. It is not inherently morally obligatory for people to have multiple children (no such command exists in the Bible and God's Word even indicates that many Christians are called to be single and not have any children at all, according to 1 Corinthians 7:7-8 and Matthew 19:12). But, it is morally permissible and lawful for parents to have multiple children, as there is nothing inherently evil about having more than one child and there is nothing inherently good about having only one child. Thus, Chinese parents were not morally obligated to obey this law since this law was invalid. When the Chinese government took legal action against parents who violated this so-called "law," it was not the parents, but the state who was in the wrong.

Although there is no inherent moral obligation for someone to immigrate to another nation, there is also nothing morally wrong with this action. Those who would venture to take this position—that immigration is evil—would be forced to condemn many of their ancestors as well as Biblical examples, such as righteous Ruth and Rahab (who both immigrated to Israel) and Mary and Joseph (who fled to Egypt as refugees). For these reasons, this position is difficult to defend and few Christians would take it. If it was not sinful for Ruth to permanently immigrate to Israel, it is not sinful for an immigrant from Mexico to permanently immigrate to America. If it was not sinful for Mary and Joseph to temporarily immigrate to Egypt as refugees from evil king Herod, then it is not wrong for a Christian family from Syria that faces persecution from radical Jihadists to immigrate to America as refugees until the evil in their home nation passes.

Furthermore, there is nothing inherently good about Ruth, the immigrant from Mexico, Mary and Joseph, or the Syrian family remaining in the nations they were born in. Doing so could result in death or great danger to them and their families or could be opposed to God's calling on their lives. If there is nothing inherently morally evil about these immigrants coming to your country and if there is nothing inherently morally good about them staying in their nations, your nation must not have laws which prohibit immigration.

Those who argue it is fine for governments to enact laws forbidding things which are morally permissible have no grounds to disagree with China's "one-child" policy. If it is acceptable for a nation to forbid or inhibit immigration, which is morally permissible, then it is acceptable for China to forbid or inhibit parents from having more than one child, which is also morally permissible. In both circumstances, these nations are exceeding the authority granted to them by God and excuse this transgression because of their perceived national interests (i.e., by saying that there are "too many" people in their nation or "not enough" jobs, land, or resources).

A KING'S GLORY

Both nations previously described believe that by enacting legislation which prevents the numbers of humans in their societies from increasing, they will bring more security and prosperity to their nations. However, such beliefs are opposed to the Word of God. According to Proverbs 14:28, "In a multitude of people is a king's glory, but in the dearth of people is a prince's ruin." It is always objectively better for a nation to have *more* people. More people work to produce more things, are able to fight to defend the nation better, and increase the collective knowledge of the nation.

Nations get into serious trouble when they decide having *less* people is better than having more people and start encouraging abortions, implementing "one-child" policies, getting involved in large unnecessary wars, or forbidding immigration. If the United States, for instance, succeeded in banning all immigration, the economy of the country would be destroyed and the people would suffer ruin. A population pyramid collapse (similar to those faced by China, South Korea, and Japan), which has already started to take shape in America, would quickly become a problem impossible to solve, since there would not be enough young people to take care of the elderly. Additionally, some of the most essential industries (agriculture, construction, healthcare, software development, for instance), which are highly dependent on immigration for labor, would implode.

Instead of focusing on suicidal anti-human policies, Christian nations should be wise and pro-human by trying to increase the number of humans in their nations as much as possible. This will have the added benefit of allowing Christians in the nation to preach the gospel to as many people as possible. Satan would prefer for every country to be like North Korea—completely closed off to the world—so he can keep its people in darkness and safe from hearing about the Gospel. He would also like to prevent foreigners from non-Christian countries from immigrating to Christian countries; he has lost millions of souls to God because of this over the course of human history, even during the time of Israel, when foreigners were rescued from darkness and given a place among the people of Israel in God's Temple (Isaiah 56:6-7).

THE BOUNDARIES OF NATIONS

One of the only Biblical objections to immigration comes from Acts 17:26, which says,

> He made from one man every nation of mankind to live on all the face of the earth, having determined their appointed times and the boundaries of their habitation.

This verse is frequently twisted to mean people cannot immigrate from their home nations because there are boundaries that God has established for their nations and that doing so destroys the nations God has created. To those who read this verse without preconceived agendas, this is obviously not the point this verse is trying to convey, especially when it is read in context.

If that was the correct interpretation, it would mean all of the Europeans who left the bounds of their nations and immigrated to America (which was inhabited by Native American nations) violated the boundaries that

God had given to them. What should be done about that? To make it right, should all the descendants of these Europeans be deported back to their nations of origin? If your ancestors were British and you live in America, should you be sent back to Britain? What if half of your ancestors were British and half were German? Should half of you get deported to Britain and half to Germany? This is obviously insane, since there has been an incomprehensible amount of national boundary shifting, immigration, and ethnicity and culture mixing throughout human history.

The plain and proper way to interpret this verse is to say that God is the author of history and He is creating a beautiful story. He planned for some British and other European peoples to leave their home nations and travel to America and, because of that, a new American nation and many beautiful American lives and families were created and brought into existence. My wife, my children, and I would not exist if it wasn't for immigrants who left their national boundaries. God is doing the same thing with Hispanic peoples who are immigrating to the United States right now. God is using them to create beautiful new nations, ethnicities, languages, families, and human lives as a part of His divine plan. This is wonderful and we should rejoice and praise God for it, just as much for Hispanic immigrants who are coming to the U.S. as we do for our European ancestors who came here.

YOU ALSO WERE STRANGERS

On a related note, the reason God repeatedly gives for why foreigners and immigrants must be treated with equality in Exodus 23:9 is cutting: "You yourselves know the feelings of a stranger, for you also were strangers in the land of Egypt." Every human on earth is descended from immigrants and people who were considered to be "foreigners" at some point in history. In America, for instance, the people who speak out the loudest against foreigners and immigration are themselves descendants of foreigners and immigrants. Many of these people are the descendants of Irish and Italian immigrants who were treated as despicably as they now treat others who they perceive as "foreigners." They should know better.

In some far right circles, it is common for sinful men to tell even second or third generation citizens of Mexican, Indian, or African descent to "go back to your own kind" and speak gleefully about the future national deportation of immigrants. But, if a national deportation of all people who were not native to America were to be carried out, all the people who are arguing for it (who are usually of Irish, German, British, Italian, Scandinavian or other European descent) would need to be deported back to their countries of origin as well, leaving only the Native Americans. If one of these men objected to this by saying, "My family has been in America for three hundred years, while your family has been here for only thirty years," he would be susceptible to the same argument from a Native American who could say, "My family has been here for three thousand years, while your family has been here for only three hundred years." Ultimately, the length of time a foreigner or his family have resided in a nation does not change a Christian nation's obligation under the law of God to treat him equally.

THE FREELOADER IMMIGRANT OBJECTION

Although God's law is clear on treating foreigners equally and that should be sufficient for a faithful Christian, there are many pragmatic objections to God's command which should be dealt with. The first such objection is that "foreigners just come here and mooch off our welfare, take our jobs, commit crime, and contribute to the moral decline of our nation!"

First, in a Christian nation, ideally, there should be no government welfare system or handouts at all (for immigrants or for natives), as Christians are instructed to provide for themselves, their families, and the poor out of their own pocket (Ephesians 4:28, 1 Thessalonians 4:11, and 1 Timothy 5:8), a responsibility which nowhere in the Bible is delegated to the government. That objection should be a non-issue, since it is ultimately a complaint about the welfare system, not immigration.

Regarding the "taking our jobs" issue, in a Christian nation, employers should generally be free to hire whoever they want to hire. It is a sign that socialism has crept into a government when they monkey with economic forces by forbidding companies to hire certain candidates from the potential labor pool. When socialistic governments create unnatural economic conditions, a moral hazard will always ensue. If citizens of Western nations are not forced to compete with foreigners for jobs, they will become lazier and more entitled than they currently are. They need more competition, not less, to become more honest, hard-working, and committed to improving their education again.

When it comes to the crime and moral degradation problem, Christian nations should obey God's Law by outlawing violence, oppression, and degeneracy and should swiftly and appropriately punish violations of these offenses. Those who are justly convicted murderers or child rapists should be executed regardless of whether the murderer or child rapist is a foreigner or a native. Likewise, those who are justly convicted thieves should be required to pay back restitution to their victims regardless of whether the thief is a foreigner or a native. Whatever the offense, those convicted of crimes should be swiftly punished, regardless of whether they are foreigners or natives, in keeping with Ecclesiastes 8:11, which warns about the dangers of delayed punishment. In a Christian nation, the crime issue should not be a problem. Foreigners who are in criminal gangs or inclined to violence or degeneracy will not even desire to come to a Christian nation because of the nation's reputation for punishing the wicked.

THE LIMITED RESOURCES OBJECTION

Others may object to the expectation that immigrants be welcomed and treated equally by claiming there isn't enough room in their country for more people, and limited resources make it impossible to support them. This objection is the exact same propaganda used by Communist China when it implemented its anti-human "one-child" policy. It is also the same line used by population control proponents across the world. But those who make such claims, whether they are Communists, population-control proponents, abortion supporters, or those opposed to immigration and foreigners, rarely ever substantiate this assumption.

In the United States alone, there are *millions* of square miles of land which are completely uninhabited and empty, so there is no lack of space. When it comes to resources, America (and the world as a whole) has an incomprehensible amount of untapped resources (farm land, minerals, water, metals, oil, coal, etc.). To extract these resources, more hardworking humans are needed. Thus, to extract its abundant supply of resources, a nation should implement pro-human policies which encourage high birth rates, large families, and more immigration. Ironically, pursuing population control measures will result in a natural resource crisis, like the one China is experiencing, or like the one the United States will experience if we succeed in kicking out all of the hardworking immigrants. This makes perfect sense, given the previously quoted admonition of Proverbs 14:28, “In a multitude of people is a king’s glory, but in the dearth of people is a prince’s ruin.”

THE LIBERAL IMMIGRANT VOTE OBJECTION

Another common objection is, "All those foreigners are going to vote for godless, anti-Christian liberals!" In response to this statement, it is important to first ask the question: why do foreigners typically vote for liberals? Immigrants from third-world countries often have traditional family values and are very religious (most commonly, very Christian), making them statistically more likely to be attracted to conservatism. They frequently are repulsed by liberal positions on sexuality and socialism, since many of these immigrants are traditional Christians who escaped from socialist countries.

However, conservatives across the Western world have foolishly chosen to alienate this potential massive voter base by constantly threatening to deport them. It makes sense that immigrants tend to vote for liberals, even though they have nothing in common. If conservatives stop threatening to deport people who should be their supporters, they might have more supporters.

Second, it must be emphasized that the Law of God does not require nations to give foreigners a right to serve in political office or vote in elections immediately upon their entry into the country. Regarding the king of the Israelites, Deuteronomy 17:14-15 says,

> When you enter the land which the LORD your God gives you, and you possess it and live in it, and you say, 'I will set a king over me like all the nations who are around me,' you shall surely set a king over you whom the LORD your God chooses, one from among your countrymen you shall set as king over yourselves; you may not put a foreigner over yourselves who is not your countryman.

As a side note, it is important to point out that God is not instructing the Israelites to have a king in this passage. In fact, God specifically condemns the Israelites for giving their power to a king and rejecting God as their king in the process (1 Samuel 8). Rather, in this passage, God simply foretells that the Israelites *will* choose to give themselves a king and then He gives some requirements that this king must meet, one of which is that he must not be a foreigner.

In democratic nations (which do not have kings), this verse should be applied by excluding foreigners from serving as lawmakers and voters until they have officially joined the nation. However, according to Exodus 12:48, foreigners must be allowed to join themselves to the nation and become as natives after meeting certain religious criteria which are not burdensome:

> But if a stranger sojourns with you, and celebrates the Passover to the LORD, let all his males be circumcised, and then let him come near to celebrate it; and he shall be like a native of the land.

This happened many times in the Old Testament, with Moses' wife (a Midianite), Rahab (a Canaanite), Ruth (a Moabite), Uriah (a Hittite), and in the story of Esther when many people (who were Persians) became Jews. Notice that these individuals became fully joined to the Israelite nation while also retaining the national identity of their birth (for instance, Uriah was called

"Uriah the Hittite," in 2 Samuel 23:39), meaning that it was possible for these individuals to belong to two nations simultaneously. Another Biblical example of this was the Apostle Paul, who was simultaneously a Jew and a Roman, according to Acts 21:39 and Acts 22:27. Also notice that these individuals were able to join themselves to the Israelite nation quickly, within their own lifetimes, after meeting only a few criteria. In the case of the Persians who became Jews (Esther 8:17), this process appears to have happened very swiftly.

Although the religious criteria for joining the nation of Israel will be different from the criteria needed to join a Christian nation, whatever these criteria are should be simple and easy to meet in a few years or less. The requirements must not be arbitrary and sinfully partial (i.e., you have to be of a certain ancestry or have a certain skin color) or so cumbersome that it is practically or actually impossible for a foreigner to become a citizen (i.e., a large sum of money is required to buy citizenship, only doctors or other highly skilled individuals are allowed to become citizens, or a foreigner's grandchildren can become citizens, but he can't), since this would contradict the examples found in God's Word.

Instead, the criteria for citizenship, however they are delineated, should ensure that foreigners who desire to gain full voting and political participation rights profess the Christian faith and demonstrate a commitment to integrating into the Christian church and the national community. This does not mean that they must renounce other citizenship they hold or forsake all elements of their other nationality, as Paul's example of being a Jew and Roman simultaneously illustrates.

In my opinion, criteria which would mirror those found in Ezekiel 12:48, but tailored for a Christian nation, would include requiring an affidavit from the prospective citizen which affirms that he or she professes the Christian faith and its core doctrines (which, among other tenets, naturally includes a belief in objective morality founded in God's Word) and has been baptized. Additionally, there should be evidence that the prospective citizen regularly attends church in the nation and participates in communion with other believers there. Furthermore, evidence of participation in national holidays could be used to demonstrate integration into the national community.

Foreigners who reside in the nation but do not meet these requirements can still reside in the nation and must be treated the same as anyone else, but they should not participate in the political process until they meet the criteria and join the nation as a citizen. In a Christian nation, foreigners who are not Christians, who do not believe in the morality prescribed by the Bible, and who are not integrated into the national community or the Christian church would not be allowed to vote, thus nullifying the objection that they will be any more likely to vote for wicked politicians than any other Christian native would be.

THE BORDER SECURITY OBJECTION

"Well isn't border security a good thing? Shouldn't we know who is coming into the country?"

I have not disputed this. It is possible to have border security (which includes border walls and armed guards) and know who is coming into the nation while treating foreigners fairly and allowing immigration. The book of Nehemiah describes how the Jews built a wall around Jerusalem under the clear hand of God (Nehemiah 2:17-18) and were willing to defend themselves and their people with weapons (Nehemiah 4:13-14, 16) from foreign military invaders who were conspiring against them (Nehemiah 4:7-8). There is nothing wrong with this.

Legitimate military invaders and spies from foreign nations can be prevented from entering a nation while obeying God's Law. Bona fide members of terrorist organizations, cartels, and criminal gangs would also fit into the category of military invaders and spies. On the other hand, those with criminal pasts who have clearly turned their lives around and repented of their sins should not be prohibited from entering the nation and even from joining it. Rahab was permitted to join the nation of Israel, even though she was a Canaanite prostitute and, likely, a pimp (she was an unmarried woman who appears to have owned a house where prostitution was performed, according to Joshua 2).

It is important to note, however, that a nation cannot label all foreigners and immigrants as "military invaders" or "spies" unless these men are true military invaders or spies. During World War II, it was evil for the United States to consider Japanese (or Japanese-looking) persons to be spies. Because of this designation, the U.S. government took the only logical action that comes from making such a declaration: to unjustly lock all these people up in camps.

This is the only logical outcome of labeling entire people groups as military invaders or spies. If, in an unspoken attempt to curb their immigration, all Chinese nationals (or Chinese-looking people) are considered to be military invaders and spies, what should be done with the Chinese people already in your nation? Logically, it should be presumed that they are also military invaders and spies. What do you do with military invaders and spies who have entered your nation? Put them in prison camps. And, if a particularly far-right or far-left politician is in power, the final solution might just be to execute all of them.

Our God will not be mocked. A nation cannot cheat its way out of obeying His Law. God knows the hearts and intentions of men, and will not accept it when a nation does horrible things to foreigners, violating His Law, because the nation decided to brand all the foreigners as spies and invaders. Those who violate God's Law in ways they consider to be small and insignificant—by preventing foreigners from entering their nation, deporting them, or otherwise denying equal rights to them—will soon start violating God's Law in more horrifying ways: by genociding entire people groups. Sin is always a slippery slope. When a person or a nation compromises with Satan in small ways, the prince of darkness will certainly use this leverage to take greater advantage of them.

THE SLIPPERY SLOPE OF GENOCIDE

If someone is opposed to immigration but thinks he could never be driven to murderous, genocidal madness because he is too good for that, it would be beneficial for him to read Christopher Browning's *Ordinary Men: Reserve Police Battalion 101 and the Final Solution in Poland.* This book describes normal men who had families, small businesses, and were

Christians and patriots, but who rounded up and shot Jewish families in the woods. Although most of these men were not radicals or ideologues, living through decades of propaganda about Jewish foreigners made it easier for them to fall to peer pressure and engage in mass murder of fellow image bearers of God, including children. If someone continues to compromise with sin, rejecting God's Law and putting patriotism and politics over the Word of God, he will end up doing the same things these men did, if given the opportunity. And because of increasingly violent rhetoric from anti-immigration influencers today, it is quite possible that he will indeed get this opportunity to choose between obeying God's Law and genociding his neighbors.

In a September 2025 X post, C. Jay Engel, a self-described "Heritage American" and Christian political influencer, stated that he believes violence and breaking the law, including suspending the U.S. Constitution, is needed to handle the problem of non-Heritage Americans:

> …If we want to reverse this stuff, technical mechanisms like deportations and remigration and

immigration caps are not what is required. That's misleading.

It would have been true in 2000. But it's 2025. If you want to reverse this stuff, you have to redefine the Postwar Consensus definition on things like unbounded religious liberty, absolutist individual rights, and a universalist version of equal representation. You have to ignore the legal edifice of the postwar federal framework.

These are US citizens in Dearborn. You would have to denaturalize, strip people of their citizenship, forcibly remove them from their second and third generation homes. It would require violence. You'd have to ignore courts and local political authorities, retroactively apply new laws—these laws wouldn't come from legislation—they would be executive orders (not laws). They would be standards of executive fiat.

It would require a post-Constitutional order, even if the intention was to only suspend it temporarily, to get back to the Constitutional norms. No one in Washington is willing to do any of this.

To the extent that we are not honest with ourselves, to that extent American heritage will be gone in a few years. It is true that we are "losing our country." But we are losing it legally, within the permitted legal framework of the American system.

We would rather live the lie, remain in reputational good standing, live up to "our ideals," than save our country. Saving our country would imply all sorts of human, constitutional, financial, reputational casualties. It wouldn't just be uncomfortable like opposing the COVID regime; there would be an onslaught of intense and gut wrenching guilt, a burden of carrying history on one's shoulders. None of these burdens are worth it. Our country and its heritage just isnt [sic] worth it.[15]

---

[15] Engel, C. (2025, September 5). *We are not being honest. If we want to reverse this stuff, technical mechanisms like deportations and remigration and immigration...* [Post]. X. https://x.com/contramordor/status/1963949895393345978

> This is not a doom post. This is a face reality and do something about it post. This is a do what is required, and you can avoid the fate laid out post.[16]

Thomas Achord, a Christian teacher and author of *Who Is My Neighbor? An Anthology In Natural Relations* who was a panelist at Joel Webbon's 2025 Trashworld conference,[17] added this to the conversation:

> I don't advocated [sic] deportations. They won't achieve the goal at which people are aiming. History and travel prove this.
>
> What conservatives/MAGAs/rightists want will require bloodshed, violence, aggression, brutality on mass scale. Not arrests, deportations, and paperwork. War.
>
> A more ethnically and politically united U.S. in the 1800s tried to deport Africans but failed due to logistics, even though they had way

[16] Engel, C. (2025, September 5). *This is not a doom post. This is a face reality and do something about it post. This is a...* [Post]. X. https://x.com/contramordor/status/1964009529684660229

[17] Stevenson, B. (2025, May 5). So, I Went to See the Christian Nationalists... (Part 2). Letters to My Friends. https://bobstevenson.substack.com/p/so-i-went-to-see-the-christian-nationalists-6a8

more will and unity on the issue and way less people to deport than we do today.

We today have more tech/transportation means but not the hardened will and unity of mind to do the dirty deed. We are also dealing not with a few million powerless slaves but +55 million well-entrenched people. Basically several nations of peoples would need to be violently uprooted and brutally dispersed in a short period of time.

And you'd have to silence/combat liberals and their NGOs, politicians, academia, and especially their media organs due to all the ensuing pain, wailing, crimes, hatred, violence. You'd then need to ensure that those deported people, their descendants, their criminal/gang organizations, and their formal nations never ever ever retaliate against the U.S. or its citizens at home or abroad - for generations and generations.

Basically, what people are wanting today would require a blitz total war on +55 million people, followed by sustained imperial global power.[18]

If our nation does not repent and turn back to God, striving to do what He commands us to do, I fear that the rise of such godless sentiments will indeed result in great violence and bloodshed in the future. The only way this can be stopped is if godly men and women across the country decide they will no longer compromise with this sin and the wolves who promote it. Instead, they must obey God's Law and teach others to do the same, as Christ instructs us to do (Matthew 5:19).

BORDER SECURITY IN A CHRISTIAN NATION

Returning to the "border security" objection against immigration, the astute reader will note that, while this book advocates for permitting immigration and castigates those who would deport or treat immigrants

[18] Achord, T. (2025, September 5). *I don't advocated deportations. They won't achieve the goal at which people are aiming. History and travel prove this. What...* [Post]. X. https://x.com/ThomasAchord/status/1964086502880694524

unfairly, nowhere does this chapter decry the concept of border security.

These things are not mutually exclusive. It is possible to simultaneously have strong borders, encourage immigration, and treat foreigners fairly. According to the Biblical model, a nation can (and, when threatened, should) have border fortifications and armed border guards who will defend the nation from foreign military personnel and spies. Anyone who wishes to enter the nation should be required to check in at official points where background checks can be conducted on foreigners to determine whether they are regular foreigners (tourists, workers, refugees, etc.) or likely to be legitimate military invaders and spies. In the digital age with incredible biometric technology, there is no reason why these background checks should take longer than a couple of hours in 95% of cases.

A Christian nation should have a strong foreign intelligence agency which competently spies on hostile nations and keeps track of all known adversarial foreign military personnel and spies. Watchlists of known hostile foreign military personnel, spies, terrorists, and cartel and gang members should be kept and added to the background check system, in the same way many nations around the world already do this. Foreign military invaders and spies can be denied entry to the nation. Or, if the nation is familiar with Sun Tzu's *The Art of War*, they will allow them in but attempt to turn the invaders or spies into reverse spies, or coax them into surrendering without a fight by offering them good treatment. Regular foreigners, on the other hand, must be allowed in, in accordance with God's Law.

If there are any failures with this system, they will be failures with the foreign intelligence agency and not with the immigration of foreigners in general, which is protected by the Law of God. If a background check fails to detect that a foreigner is a spy, the problem is that your nation has a weak intelligence agency, not that it allows foreigners into the nation.

However, even the strongest intelligence and border security systems will fail and spies will enter the nation. North Korea and the former German Democratic Republic (East Germany) are two nations with some of the strongest intelligence apparatuses and borders ever known to man. But spies have still managed to get into both of these nations, despite their strong borders and intelligence agencies. Although nations should try to stop spies from entering, they should not stress about it to the point of violating the Law of God, since it is impossible to stop all spies from entering anyways.

Additionally, even with excellent border security, there may be some innocuous foreigners who enter by jumping a border fence or otherwise failing to submit to a background check at the designated check-in point. These individuals should be tracked down, ordered to submit to a background check, and be required to pay a reasonable fine for wasting the government's time. Since this crime is on par, in terms of severity, with trespassing or doing business as a locksmith without a government background check and license, the punishment should be similar.

God's Law requires punishment for crimes to be just, such as, "eye for eye, tooth for tooth, hand for hand, foot for foot" (Exodus 21:24). An example of an unjust punishment would be destroying the life of a political protestor who trespasses at the capitol building by locking her in a federal prison for twenty years. Although her offense certainly deserves to be punished, twenty years in prison and the complete destruction of her life is grossly excessive and evil. In the same way, if someone hops a border fence and does not initially submit to a government background check, but then proceeds to work hard for ten years in the nation, pays taxes, and does not commit any other crimes, it is unjust to destroy his life for this minor offense by deporting him and his family, removing them from their church and their friends, depriving them of the use of their property, and taking away everything they have worked hard for. Such asymmetrical punishment is characteristic of ancient, barbaric pagan nations and should never be advocated for by Christians who desire to live in a Christian nation.

The "My Ancestors Were Better" Objection

There are many who would argue the original European immigrants to America were pioneers. Unlike immigrants today, they say, the Europeans built the country and brought Christianity to a land populated by heathens. When I hear this type of claim, I always want to ask, "What did our European ancestors build?" The answer is something along the lines of, "Buildings, cities, businesses, churches, culture, governance systems, and things like that."

But this is *exactly* what immigrants today are doing in the United States. They are *literally* building this nation—our buildings, cities, businesses, churches, software programs, culture, neighborhoods, institutions, and all manner of other things that never existed before. Why is it fine for European immigrants to justify their existence by building things, but not for brown-skinned immigrants to do the same?

The objector may point to the Christianity of the European settlers in contrast with the perceived godlessness of modern immigrants. However, according to a 2024 Pew Research Center study, 70% of immigrants to North American countries (specifically, the U.S. and Canada) are Christians.[19] Meanwhile, according to a 2025 Pew Research Center study, only 62% of Americans now

---

[19] Kramer, S. and Tong, Y. (2024, August 19). The Religious Composition of the World's Migrants. Pg. 17. Pew Research Center. https://www.pewresearch.org/wp-content/uploads/sites/20/2024/08/PR_2024.08.19_religious-composition-migrants_report.pdf

identify as Christians.[20] Since the European immigrants were justified in staying in America because they were more Christian than the Native Americans, does this mean that today's immigrants to America are justified in staying as well because they are more Christian than the current inhabitants of the land? Ironically, immigrants are not only helping build America, they are also growing the Christian population. Why on earth would Christians be opposed to Christians immigrating to their country and making it even more Christian?

THE CULTURAL PRESERVATION OBJECTION

This is usually the last-ditch objection from immigration opponents, once all of their other objections have been answered. There is a fear that, if too many immigrants are allowed into a country, they will destroy the existing culture. But it is important to remember the same thing was said about the objector's ancestors.

[20] Smith, G., et al. (2025, February 26). Decline of Christianity in the U.S. Has Slowed, May Have Leveled Off. Pew Research Center. https://www.pewresearch.org/religion/2025/02/26/decline-of-christianity-in-the-us-has-slowed-may-have-leveled-off/

Americans in the early 1900's were told that Irish and Italian immigrants would destroy their culture. And when earlier Europeans arrived in America in the 1600's, 1700's, and 1800's, don't you think many Native Americans were concerned that these immigrants would eventually destroy their culture? Those Pilgrim immigrants who forever changed the culture of the Americas were refugees fleeing religious persecution in a country where the Normans had modified the culture when they invaded the Anglo-Saxons; the Anglo-Saxons had changed the culture when they invaded the Romano-Britons; and the Romans had changed the culture when they invaded the Celtic tribes.

An important thing to remember about "culture" is that it is constantly changing. Even without immigration, the culture of a nation will always be in a persistent state of change. In the United States, jazz, rap, and rock-and-roll music, which significantly changed culture, were not created by immigrants; they were created by Americans who had lived in the nation for generations. Other elements of cultural change which Americans started include fast food, baby showers, Thanksgiving, the mid-century modern architectural style, and American football.

Additionally, there is no moral significance to culture change in itself. When a nation becomes more sinful, that is an evil change. But there is nothing morally significant about whether a culture changes by incorporating more Spanish loanwords into its language, more Mexican food into its culinary preferences, or more twenty-inch rims on its cars. All of these things are morally neutral. On what objective moral grounds can someone assert that cultures must be static and never change? Such a reason cannot be found anywhere in the Word of God or using basic logic. It would be absurd for someone to say that vanilla ice cream is their preferred flavor and no other flavors should be invented or allowed in society. Ultimately, the dislike of cultural change is the same thing. It is nothing more than a personal preference which has no objective bearing on anyone else.

WHAT IS REALLY BEHIND OBJECTIONS TO IMMIGRATION?

When we dissect and expose all the contradictory and illogical arguments used by those opposed to foreigners and immigration, all that is left is sinful racial and ethnic partiality, condemned by James 2:9. In the end, there are no true, logical, or consistent anti-foreigner or anti-immigrant arguments other than "they look different than me" or "they act differently than me." Are all people who are opposed to immigration and the equal treatment of foreigners racists? Absolutely not. Most of them have simply been indoctrinated by decades of propaganda from politicians, influencers, and news outlets and have never thought seriously about their position on this topic or examined its pernicious roots.

Notwithstanding, many who are opposed to immigration would wholeheartedly agree with the quote presented at the beginning of this chapter, which now appears in its entirety:

> France to the French, England to the English, America to the Americans, and Germany to the

> Germans. We are resolved to prevent the settlement in our country of a strange people [Jewish strangers] which was capable of snatching for itself all the leading positions in the land, and to oust it… Above all, German culture, as its name alone shows, is German and not Jewish, and therefore its management and care will be entrusted to members of our own nation… I think that the sooner this problem is solved the better; for Europe cannot settle down until the Jewish question is cleared up.[21]

If it wasn't obvious, this statement was made by Adolf Hitler in 1939. The types of arguments that Hitler used to decry the Jewish "strangers" are still used, almost verbatim, by influential pundits who are opposed to immigration today. Until recently, it was more common for them to say these things in regards to Mexicans, Central Americans, Indians, and Black people. With increasing frequency, however, they are starting to say the exact same things about the Jews again too.

---

[21] Extract from the Speech by Adolf Hitler, January 30, 1939. (n.d.). Yad Vashem, The World Holocaust Remembrance Center. https://www.yadvashem.org/docs/extract-from-hitler-speech.html

THE RESPONSIBILITY OF A RIGHTEOUS NATION

If someone finds himself agreeing with Adolf Hitler's sentiments in this speech, he might just be the "baddie" here when it comes to foreigners and immigration. But, later in the same speech, Hitler did get one thing right. He correctly pointed out that the United States was hypocritical for criticizing Hitler's policy towards the Jews while being unwilling to accept Jewish immigrants itself. For instance, in 1939, the *St. Louis*, a ship full of Jewish immigrants trying to escape Nazi Germany was denied entry at its planned destination, Cuba, after a right-wing newspaper helped whip up an anti-immigrant and anti-Jewish frenzy in the nation, putting pressure on local officials to prohibit the foreign Jews from disembarking at the port.

The ship then anchored off the coast of Miami (close enough to see the lights of the city) and pleaded with the United States for refuge. Under pressure from voters who were hostile towards immigrants during the

Great Depression, the U.S. government ignored the request and the ship was then forced to return to Western Europe, where 254 of the ship's 937 passengers were captured by the Nazis and killed in the Holocaust.[22] The blood of these passengers is not only on the hands of the Nazis, but also on the Cuban and U.S. government officials and voters who refused to save them in accordance with the precepts of the Law of God.

Proverbs 24:11 commands, "Deliver those who are being taken away to death, and those who are staggering to slaughter, oh hold them back." Likewise, Psalm 82:4 states, "Rescue the weak and needy; deliver them out of the hand of the wicked." If a nation has the ability to rescue immigrants who face likely death due to crime, hunger, or persecution in a foreign land, do these verses not apply to it? Proverbs 31:8-9 also admonishes kings, "Open your mouth for the mute, for the rights of all the unfortunate. Open your mouth, judge righteously, and defend the rights of the afflicted and needy." Was President Franklin Delano Roosevelt expected to obey

---

[22] Voyage of the St. Louis. (2024, June 18). United States Holocaust Memorial Museum.
https://encyclopedia.ushmm.org/content/en/article/voyage-of-the-st-louis

this command when he decided whether to admit the ship full of Jewish refugees? Surely he was.

Ezekiel 16:49-50 comments,

> Behold, this was the guilt of your sister Sodom: she and her daughters had arrogance, abundant food and careless ease, but she did not help the poor and needy. Thus they were haughty and committed abominations before Me. Therefore I removed them when I saw it.

Although Sodom has a more famous sin that also brought the judgment of God upon them, God specifically points to their refusal to help the poor and needy as a reason for their destruction. Does this passage not perfectly describe America and many Western nations? Can America, a nation which is rich, but refuses Jewish immigrants and sends them to their deaths, expect to escape judgement any more than Sodom, if she does not repent? Absolutely not.

DO NO VIOLENCE TO THE FOREIGNER

Recently, Joel Webbon made the following statement, which highlights the moral depravity of many of those who are opposed to immigration:

> For America for the next twenty to fifty years, there should be virtually zero immigration… And I'm not talking about illegal; I'm talking about legal. No immigration… We need a wall, this is merciful, by the way. I'm not just trying to be unhinged. We need a wall. We need guys on that wall, standing on top of that wall, and if someone starts to approach the wall, there needs to be a warning, 'Back away.' If they don't listen to the warning, they need to be shot. They need to be killed. [...] That will be the more merciful option because what will end up happening is you'll have a handful of people that get killed and then thousands of people that don't experience the misery of coming and then having to be removed[…] That is the more merciful option. That is the way biblical justice is done. One is

> punished and the rest stand in fear. That's the Bible's model.[23]

This horrifying quote reminds me of Proverbs 12:10, which states, "But even the compassion of the wicked is cruel." Saying that it is compassionate, or "merciful," to kill a human so that he doesn't experience misery later in life or bring misery to others is the exact same argument that many abortion supporters use to justify their willingness to kill the pre-born. Truly, the "mercy" of the wicked is exceedingly cruel.

Despite claiming that his view is Biblical, Webbon is saying to do the exact opposite of what the Bible commands in passages like Jeremiah 22:3, which says,

> Thus says the LORD, "Do justice and righteousness, and deliver the one who has been robbed from the power of his oppressor. Also do not mistreat or do violence to the stranger [other translations also translate this as "foreigner" or

[23] Mantyla, K. (2024, November 14). 'They Need To Be Killed': Joel Webbon Says Anyone Trying To Cross The Border Must Be Shot. People for the American Way. https://www.peoplefor.org/rightwingwatch/they-need-be-killed-joel-webbon-says-anyone-trying-cross-border-must-be-shot

> "alien"], the orphan, or the widow; and do not shed innocent blood in this place."

Likewise, Zechariah 7:9-10 states,

> Thus has the LORD of hosts said, "Dispense true justice and practice kindness and compassion each to his brother; and do not oppress the widow or the orphan, the stranger [or "foreigner," "alien," or "sojourner"] or the poor; and do not devise evil in your hearts against one another."

Isaiah 59:7 says, "Their feet run to evil, and they hasten to shed innocent blood; their thoughts are thoughts of iniquity, devastation and destruction are in their highways," which is a perfect description of violent men who advocate for gunning down poor immigrants, most of whom are Christians, to make an example out of them. The church must thoroughly purge itself from such murderous, wicked false teachers.

When Mary, Joseph, and baby Jesus fled as refugees from King Herod to Egypt, even pagan Egypt (as evil as it was) did not have a policy to kill everyone who tried to cross the border into their nation. We should praise God for this and a Christian nation should never seek to become even more evil than pagan Egypt. Similarly, we can praise God that Ruth was allowed to cross the border into Israel and join the nation without a border guard hacking her to bits to "make an example" out of her. Because even the rebellious Israelites were not as foolish or violent as today's political pundits, there were no laws prohibiting or capping immigration and we are not aware of anyone advocating for murdering people who tried to cross the border. Ruth was permitted to immigrate to Israel and she was not a curse to the nation (an attitude which many today have towards foreigners), but was a great blessing, being in the bloodline of both King David and the Messiah.

Treating Others as Yourself

Matthew 7:12 states, "In *everything* [emphasis added], therefore, treat people the same way you want them to treat you, for this is the Law and the Prophets." If you and your family lived somewhere where your lives were constantly threatened by persecution, hunger, or crime, wouldn't you try to escape to a country that was safe for your family, instead of staying put and watching them die? And if you had to do this, would you want all the safe countries where you could flee to deny entry to all immigrants and to have shoot-to-kill orders for anyone trying to cross the border? If your answer is "no," then the Law of God requires you to oppose such evil policies. If you fail to obey it, that is sin. In *everything*, you must treat people in the same way you want them to treat you.

Obviously, when it comes to treating others the way that you would want them to treat you, this must be done in alignment with the express will of God. For example, a Christian governor should not pardon or grant clemency to a justly convicted child murderer, even if he would want to be pardoned in the same situation. God has made it known that He desires criminals like this to be executed for their crimes (Genesis 9:6). But, as we have seen in this chapter, God's Law requires us to treat foreigners as equals to the native born, to protect these poor people, and to save the innocent from death.

If you still believe that all safe countries should deny asylum to immigrants, you should be very careful, because God may give you what you want. When those who have been shown great mercy refuse to be merciful, God often punishes such wicked servants in very humiliating ways (Matthew 18:21-35). Those with great wealth, safety, and religious freedom who are the biggest opponents of immigration and treating foreigners equally may someday lose their riches, be persecuted as a result of their religion or for refusing to comply with a mandate, and be forced to flee to a safer place. If this happens, will anyone want to take them in?

CHAPTER IV

RIGHT TO INTERRACIAL MARRIAGE

When I first decided to write this book, I never anticipated needing to write a section explaining that a Christian nation must protect interracial marriages in accordance with the Law of God and the examples found in the Bible. However, a new breed of dangerous wolves have recently infiltrated the church and one of their many deviant teachings is that interracial marriages are sinful and ought to be outlawed in a Christian nation. Corey Mahler, a Maryville, Tennessee attorney and Christian political influencer who hosted the influential right-wing podcast, Stone Choir, has taught the following on the subject:

> Interracial marriage is tantamount to murder. And this remains true regardless of how much our

elites, pastorate, and other degenerates fetishize and promote it.[24]

The psychophysiological response to seeing an interracial couple is similar to the (male) psychophysiological response to seeing a sodomite 'couple'—and both are similar to the psychophysiological response to seeing maggot-infested decaying flesh.[25]

As a Christian, if you do not oppose interracial unions, then you must explain precisely how God was wrong to give man this particular instinct, for all of our instincts come from God. If you believe there is nothing wrong with interracial unions, then you accuse God of sin.[26]

---

[24] Mahler, C. (2024, October 30). *Interracial marriage is tantamount to murder. And this remains true regardless of how much our elites, pastorate, and other degenerates...* [Post]. X. https://x.com/CoreyJMahler/status/1851739359495479776

[25] Mahler, C. (2024, October 7). *The psychophysiological response to seeing an interracial couple is similar to the (male) psychophysiological response to seeing a sodomite 'couple'...* [Post]. X. https://x.com/CoreyJMahler/status/1843474020722978854

[26] Mahler, C. (2024, October 7). *As a Christian, if you do not oppose interracial unions, then you must explain precisely how God was wrong to...* [Post]. X. https://x.com/CoreyJMahler/status/1843476669094408543

> Most [Americans] are still repulsed by the very idea [of interracial marriages]—viewing interracial couples much like they would rotting meat or liquid feces.[27]
>
> Under Christian Nationalism, interracial marriage will be made a capital offense.[28]

Mahler further explained his rationale for opposing interracial marriages by stating,

> I do not believe that any interracial unions (at least those that cross the major lines) are wise, but it is a matter of both wisdom and degree. For a German to marry a Dutch is typically not a problem; for a Dutch to marry an African virtually always is.
>
> There are many reasons for this. In large part, it is a matter of genetic distance and all the problems that arise from that. God built into Creation a general rule: The highest fertility is

[27] Mahler, C. (2024, September 7). *Americans lie to pollsters (same is true most places); hard data show the opposite: Most are still repulsed by the…* [Post]. X. https://x.com/CoreyJMahler/status/1832635426193932758

[28] Mahler, C. (2026, January 5). *Under Christian Nationalism, interracial marriage will be made a capital offense.* [Post]. X. https://x.com/CoreyJMahler/status/2008190202246824400

> found in unions between third or fourth cousins—any closer and you run into inbreeding depression any further and you also run into depression, but this time outbreeding depression. Where God has made His desires clear, we should not seek to violate them for the sake of personal whim (and certainly not for the sake of appeasing the world or its master below).
>
> Further, God created the races of men and interracial marriage destroys them—we should not destroy what God has created.
>
> To summarize: It is a matter, largely, of both wisdom and genetic distance.[29]

Aside from the obvious Biblical issues with these statements, they are manifestly illogical and absurd. First, I (and most normal people who are not race-obsessed weirdos) do not have a repulsive response to seeing interracial couples. In fact, I (and many other people) instinctively see these unions as beautiful. If we are assigning moral value to feelings and "instinct," who is to

---

[29] Mahler, C. (2024, December 19). *B. As noted in my answer to A, the different races of men communed with demons for different lengths of...* [Post]. X. https://x.com/CoreyJMahler/status/1869938987453816995

say whether my feelings and instincts are morally superior to Mahler's? It is inane to think your individual feelings and "instincts" are morally binding on others. There can be no foundation for morality other than the Word of God.

Second, if "all of our instincts are from God," with no distinction made between good and evil instincts, Mahler will struggle to explain why pedophiles should not act on the powerful sexual attraction and urges that they have towards children. After all, using the same logic, "all of our instincts are from God," and if you deny that God gave these instincts to pedophiles or believe that pedophilia is wrong, "then you accuse God of sin."

Third, nowhere has God "made his desires clear" that marriages with the highest possible fertility rate are morally preferable to marriages with an average fertility rate (or even marriages between infertile couples). If someone isn't fertile, does that mean there is a moral obligation for that person to be unmarried for the rest of his or her life? No, certainly not. This claim has an assumption built into it that the only morally-legitimate reason for marriage is to bear as many children as possible. These are merely Mahler's personal opinions and preferences. Who is to say that those who personally value marriage for companionship, intimacy, and enjoyment are not also correct in prioritizing these opinions and preferences?

Lastly, it is certainly true that God created the races of men. There are not different species of men, but God created various genetic differences which society considers to be significant. However, part of the way that God creates races is through interracial marriage. Why are those on the far-right trying to prevent the creation (effectively, "destroying") those beautiful new races which God is crafting as a result of interracial marriage?

Interracial Marriage in God's Law

Ultimately, however, the main problem with these sentiments is that they violate the direct commands and examples of the Bible. As mentioned and expounded on in the previous section, Leviticus 19:34 states, "The stranger who resides with you shall be to you as the native among you, and you shall love him as yourself, for you were aliens in the land of Egypt; I am the LORD your

God," and this same command is repeated in Leviticus 24:22 and Exodus 23:9. "Strangers" in the nation must be entitled to all of the same rights and privileges as the natives. This includes the ability to be joined together in any marriage which is not forbidden by the Law of God.

There are two ways the Word of God may condemn sexual unions: explicitly or implicitly. Incestuous marriages, for instance, are expressly condemned in passages like Leviticus 18:6-18. Although child marriage is prohibited less directly, it is forbidden implicitly in God's Word. Children cannot understand good and evil (Deuteronomy 1:39), indicating they do not even have the most basic level of maturity which is necessary for someone to get married. Additionally, those who get married must be physically capable of supporting themselves, as passages like Genesis 2:24 and Mark 10:7-8 indicate, something which children are not capable of. Furthermore, Ezekiel 16:7-8 stipulates that someone is only "at the time for love" after her body has reached a state of full physical maturity. Lastly, all passages referring to qualifications for marriage in the Scriptures state that the union must be between a *man* and a *woman*, and the Hebrew and Greek words used in context in these passages imply mature men and women, with words for children never being used to describe participants in marital unions. Although a minimum age for marriage is not set by the Bible, Jairus' *twelve-year-old* daughter is referred to as a "child" and "*little* girl" in Mark 5:21-43, indicating that even the age of twelve is *far* too young for marriage.

Not only does the Word of God never explicitly or implicitly condemn interracial or inter-ethnic marriage, but it provides multiple favorable examples of such unions. Since interracial unions are never forbidden in the Law, there are many examples of them found in the Scriptures, and the Law requires protecting the rights of "strangers" to marry natives, all forms of interracial and inter-ethnic marriage must be permitted in a Christian nation.

YOU SHALL NOT INTERMARRY WITH THEM

Those who are familiar with the Bible may question this claim based on the story about foreign women marrying Israelite men told in Ezra and Nehemiah. Nehemiah's account, found in 13:23-29, says,

> In those days I also saw that the Jews had married women from Ashdod, Ammon and Moab. As for their children, half spoke in the language of Ashdod, and none of them was able to speak the language of Judah, but the language of his own people. So I contended with them and cursed them and struck some of them and pulled out their hair, and made them swear by God, "You shall not give your daughters to their sons, nor take of their daughters for your sons or for yourselves. Did not Solomon king of Israel sin regarding these things? Yet among the many nations there was no king like him, and he was loved by his God, and God made him king over all Israel; nevertheless the foreign women caused even him to sin. Do we

> then hear about you that you have committed all this great evil by acting unfaithfully against our God by marrying foreign women?"

Why was Nehemiah infuriated by Israelites marrying foreign women? The answer can be found in the Law which they were violating, Deuteronomy 7:3-4, which states,

> Furthermore, you shall not intermarry with them [the Hittites, Girgashites, Amorites, Canannites, Perizzites, Hivites, and Jebusites]; you shall not give your daughters to their sons, nor shall you take their daughters for your sons. For they will turn your sons away from following Me to serve other gods; then the anger of the LORD will be kindled against you and He will quickly destroy you.

God did not want the Israelites to avoid marrying these people simply because they were foreigners; rather, as this text makes clear, He did not want intermarriage with these *specific* groups because He knew (with His perfect foreknowledge) that these people groups would lead His people astray if they intermarried, unless they repented of their sins and joined the nation of Israel first. For instance, Rahab, a Canaanite woman, repented of her sins, joined the nation of Israel, and married Salmon, an Israelite, where she became part of the bloodline of the Messiah, according to Matthew 1:5.

A SPIRITUALLY PURE PEOPLE

This command in Deuteronomy had nothing to do with preserving a *racially* "pure" Israel but rather a *spiritually* pure Israel. It cannot be referring to maintaining a racially "undefiled" nation, since God specifically made provisions for allowing foreigners (including those of other races and ethnicities) to join themselves to Israel under the Law (Exodus 12:48) and foretold of His blessing on foreigners who would do this (Isaiah 56:6-7). It is illogical to believe that a foreigner could join herself to the nation of Israel but not be able to marry an Israelite. In addition to this explicit endorsement, the Bible offers implicit approval by recounting the stories of the many foreigners who married into Israel who God blessed (Rahab, Ruth, and Asenath, for instance).

What God forbids is marrying those who He knows will lead his saints astray, spiritually defiling them. God knew that *all* of the ancient Ammonites who would marry Israelites without joining the nation of Israel or repenting of their sins would lead the Israelites they married into idolatry and sin. In Nehemiah 13:26 when it says, "nevertheless the foreign women caused even him to sin," the problem was that the foreign women caused Solomon to sin, not that they were foreign. Likewise, after Deuteronomy 7:3 forbids intermarriage with specific people groups, verse 4 gives the reason for this: "For they will turn your sons away from following Me to serve other gods; then the anger of the LORD will be kindled against you and He will quickly destroy you." The reason intermarriage was forbidden with the Ammonites is not because they were Ammonites, but because they would turn Israel's sons away from following God.

In the church age, God forbids believers from marrying those they know to be unbelievers (1 Corinthians 7:39 and 2 Corinthians 6:14) because they will lead the believers astray. However, there are no longer any nations which are off limits for interracial or inter-ethnic marriage, because all nations have been made one in Christ Jesus (Galatians 3:28 and Colossians 3:11). The gospel and the kingdom of God will advance through all nations (Matthew 24:14) and believers are free to marry those of other races or ethnicities as long as they have accepted this gospel and joined this kingdom. If you can show me a race, ethnicity, or nation of people where there is no possibility of anyone being saved, then I will concede that a believer should not marry someone of that race, ethnicity, or nation. However, this is not the case for any people, since Revelation 5:9 and 7:9 indicate that salvation will be brought to every tribe, people, nation, and tongue.

BIBLICAL EXAMPLES

To hammer home the point that Christian nations should protect the right to interracial and inter-ethnic marriages, I will briefly describe a few of these unions which God blessed in the Bible. First, Genesis 41:45 says the following about Joseph, an Israelite, "Then Pharaoh named Joseph Zaphenath-paneah; and he gave him Asenath, the daughter of Potiphera priest of On, as his wife." As far as scripture records, Joseph only had one wife, the Egyptian Asenath, and God blessed their marriage with two sons, Manasseh and Ephraim (Genesis 41:50 and 46:20). These two sons, who were half-Egyptian, went on to become the fathers of two of Israel's twelve tribes. We can see the rich blessings of God on the Israelite Joseph and the Egyptian Asenath in Genesis 41:50-52, which says:

> Now before the year of famine came, two sons were born to Joseph, whom Asenath, the daughter of Potiphera priest of On, bore to him. Joseph named the firstborn Manasseh, "For," he said, "God has made me forget all my trouble and all my father's household." He named the second Ephraim, "For," he said, "God has made me fruitful in the land of my affliction."

Rahab was a Canaanite prostitute (and, as mentioned previously, likely a pimp) from Jericho who pleased God by betraying her people to shelter and save invading Israelite spies (Joshua 2). Because of this, Rahab and her father's family were rescued from the destruction of Jericho and were joined to the nation of Israel. She married Salmon, an Israelite, and begat children. God blessed this marriage greatly by placing the Israelite Salmon and the Canaanite Rahab into the bloodlines of King David and Jesus Christ (Matthew 1:5-6, 16). Rahab is the proof that no matter how genetically different someone is, how pagan their people are, or how promiscuous and sinful they have been in their life, they can still receive the gracious gift of salvation from God. They can repent and do the right thing, become part of the people of God, join a new nation, marry another believer, and be blessed by God beyond all measure. Based on the story of Rahab alone, how could anyone ever justify the prohibition of interracial marriages by families, churches, or Christian nations? Rahab is the worst-case scenario for proponents of this unbiblical position.

Additionally, Ruth (a Moabitess) married Boaz (an Israelite, who was the descendant of Rahab and Salmon) and also entered into the Davidic and Messianic bloodline (Ruth 4:16-22). Ruth is remembered for telling Naomi,

"Your people shall be my people, and your God, my God" (Ruth 1:16), a promise which she kept, as she eventually joined the nation of Israel, was a blessing to others, and was greatly blessed by God.

MOSES' WIFE

Lastly, the story of Moses' wife is highly intriguing and serves as an important example to sinful racial partialists. Moses' first wife, Zipporah, was a Midianite (Exodus 2:15, 21-22). Later, Numbers 12:1 says that Moses married a Cushite woman. It is unclear whether Zipporah died and the Cushite woman was Moses' second marriage or whether Zipporah was the same woman, being both a Midianite and a Cushite. Perhaps her family left Cush and settled in Midian or, alternatively, she may have been mixed race, the daughter of a Cushite father and a Midianite mother.

Regardless of these fine details, however, Moses was definitely married to a Cushite woman, meaning that she was very likely Black. The vast majority of scholars believe that Cush was a nation located in modern-day

Sudan or Ethiopia, an area where the inhabitants were known for having dark skin.[30] Ezekiel 29:10 confirms Cush's location being in modern-day Sudan or Ethiopia, and Jeremiah 13:23 and Isaiah 18 describe the physical characteristics of the people of Cush in the same way as the modern Black peoples who inhabit this region. So, not only did Moses have an interracial marriage with a Cushite woman, but it is more probable than not that she was African and Black. No matter what her skin color was, genetically, she was about as distant as she could possibly get from Moses.

In light of this information, it is absurd for someone to argue that "any interracial unions that cross the major lines," like "a Dutch to marry an African," are "virtually always" unwise. The Dutch are as far genetically removed from the Cushites as the Israelites are. The Dutch are mostly descendants of Noah's son Japheth, the Israelites are mostly the descendants of Shem, and the Cushites and Africans in general are mostly the descendants of Ham. An Israelite marrying a Cushite is as genetically-diverse of an interracial marriage

[30] Davis, S. (n.d.). Cush. Bible Odyssey. https://glosbe.bibleodyssey.com/articles/cush/

as it gets after the Flood. If someone is a racial partialist who is opposed to interracial marriages, he certainly would have opposed Moses' marriage to this Cushite woman.

If someone would actually venture to condemn Moses or anyone else for their interracial marriages, Numbers 12 is written for that person. Numbers 12:1-2 states,

> Then Miriam and Aaron spoke against Moses because of the Cushite woman whom he had married (for he had married a Cushite woman); and they said, "Has the LORD indeed spoken only through Moses? Has He not spoken through us as well?" And the LORD heard it.

Although Miriam and Aaron pretended to be questioning Moses' sole authority, they were actually offended *because of the Cushite woman whom he had married*, as the text makes clear. Numbers 12:9-15 continues,

> So the anger of the LORD burned against them [Miriam and Aaron] and He departed. But when the cloud had withdrawn from over the tent,

> behold, Miriam was leprous, as white as snow. As Aaron turned toward Miriam, behold, she was leprous. Then Aaron said to Moses, "Oh, my lord, I beg you, do not account this sin to us, in which we have acted foolishly and in which we have sinned. Oh, do not let her be like one dead, whose flesh is half eaten away when he comes from his mother's womb!" Moses cried out to the LORD, saying, "O God, heal her, I pray!" But the LORD said to Moses, "If her father had but spit in her face, would she not bear her shame for seven days? Let her be shut up for seven days outside the camp, and afterward she may be received again." So Miriam was shut up outside the camp for seven days, and the people did not move on until Miriam was received again.

The fierce anger of God burns against those who hold to sinful racial and ethnic partiality, especially if this inward condition of the heart manifests itself in outward hostility towards others—regardless of whether the real reason for the hostility is made public. God knows the hearts of all men and will judge based on their secret thoughts (Romans 2:16), even if those thoughts are never vocalized. God will not let any person or nation which violates His Law in this regard go unpunished.

CHAPTER V

RIGHT TO NOT BE ENSLAVED BY ANY MAN, GOVERNMENT, OR INSTITUTION

“No slave or other person held to service or labor in any State or Territory of the Confederate States, under the laws thereof, escaping or lawfully carried into another, shall, in consequence of any law or regulation therein, be discharged from such service or labor; but shall be delivered up on claim of the party to whom such slave belongs, or to whom such service or labor may be due…

"The Confederate States may acquire new territory; and Congress shall have power to legislate and provide governments for the inhabitants of all territory belonging to the Confederate States, lying without the limits of the several states; and may permit them, at such times, and in such manner as it may by law provide, to

> form states to be admitted into the Confederacy. In all such territory, the institution of negro slavery as it now exists in the Confederate States, shall be recognized and protected by Congress, and by the territorial government: and the inhabitants of the several Confederate States and Territories, shall have the right to take to such territory any slaves lawfully held by them in any of the states or territories of the Confederate states."
>
> - Constitution of the Confederate States of America

In a nation which is obedient to God's Law, there is zero tolerance for kidnapping or chattel slavery. According to Exodus 21:16, "He who kidnaps a man, whether he sells him or he is found in his possession, shall surely be put to death." This offense also applies to human traffickers who use threats, intimidation, or other forms of persuasion to coerce humans to be trafficked for the purpose of prostitution or labor. If anyone is justly convicted of this crime, the Law of God is clear that the offender must be executed.

Every human being who has ever lived is so precious to God that He died for them (1 John 2:2). God made us in His image (Genesis 1:27) and purchased us with His own blood (1 Corinthians 6:20, 7:23, Ephesians 1:14, and 2 Peter 2:1) and, because of this, God alone owns us (Luke 20:24-25, 2 Corinthians 1:22, Ephesians 1:4, 1 Peter 2:9). He is our Master and we are His possession. Every act of kidnapping or keeping someone in a state of chattel slavery is an attempt to steal something from God that is so precious to Him that He was willing to die for it. It is an offense that rightly deserves the burning wrath of God and execution by the state.

SLAVERY IN THE LAW

Chattel slavery is not permitted in the Law of God under any circumstances. Chattel slavery is a system of enslavement where slaves have no or very few rights, cannot escape their enslavement, and are treated as the absolute property of another human. Many people who are not very familiar with the Bible claim that this form of slavery existed under the Law. It is true that this type of slavery existed in pagan nations during the time of the

Bible and is featured in some stories, but it is never permitted by the Law or condoned in the Word of God.

Although the Law does permit a form of slavery to exist, it has nothing in common with chattel slavery and more closely resembles modern-day contract employment. Under the Law, people could only become slaves voluntarily (Exodus 21:16); their masters had to provide everything (food, shelter, clothing, security, and medical treatment) for them and the slaves had numerous rights (Exodus 21); and people could only serve as slaves for a maximum time period of seven years (Exodus 21:2, Deuteronomy 15:12, and Jeremiah 34:14), although this time period could be extended for the rest of the life of the slave if the slave voluntarily requested this (Deuteronomy 15:16-17 and Leviticus 25:46).

Most importantly, a slave could choose to leave and escape from his master at any time and, after doing this, the Law forbade him from being returned to his master. He was permitted to live as a free man, consequence-free, and with no stipulations, according to Deuteronomy 23:15-16, which states:

> You shall not hand over to his master a slave who has escaped from his master to you. He shall live with you in your midst, in the place which he shall choose in one of your towns where it pleases him; you shall not mistreat him.

In fact, after this happened, if the slave's master tried to recover the escaped slave and force him back into slavery against his will, he would not only be violating this Law, but also the prohibition on kidnapping (Exodus 21:16), making him worthy of receiving the death penalty. Clearly, Biblical "slavery" is not at all like the abominable form of chattel slavery that existed in the United States, was protected by the Constitution of the Confederate States, and has been practiced in many pagan nations throughout history.

SLAVERY TO THE GOVERNMENT

It is also morally detestable and a violation of the Law of God for a nation to conscript its residents for forced military or labor service against their will. Just like individuals, governments are required to obey the Law of

God and this includes the command to not kidnap (Exodus 21:16). Just as it is evil for a government to violate the command not to murder by genociding an entire race of people, it is evil for a government to violate the command not to kidnap by conscripting its population. If the government drags innocent residents away from their homes and families and forces them to fight or work for the government against their will, there is no other word for this than kidnapping, which is forbidden by the Law.

The government may conduct a census and establish a registry of fighting-age individuals (Numbers 1:2-3). In times of national emergency, the Law implies that the government can call-up, summon, or assemble the nation's fighting age individuals (Deuteronomy 20:5-9). However, the government cannot force these individuals into actually fighting or working for the government against their will, since this would be kidnapping and involuntary slavery of innocent persons.

Nations which partake in this wickedness are characteristically pagan and totalitarian. Samuel spoke of forced conscription as a dreadful, evil thing when he warned the Israelites of the consequences if they demanded a king like the pagan nations around them, as seen in 1 Samuel 8:11-15 and 18, which states,

> This will be the procedure of the king who will reign over you: he will take your sons and place them for himself in his chariots and among his horsemen and they will run before his chariots. He will appoint for himself commanders of thousands and of fifties, and some to do his plowing and to reap his harvest and to make his weapons of war and equipment for his chariots. He will also take your daughters for perfumers and cooks and bakers. [...] Then you will cry out in that day because of your king whom you have chosen for yourselves, but the LORD will not answer you in that day.

Not only are nations forbidden from forcing their residents into conscription, but there are also five categories of individuals who specifically cannot fight for the nation even if they wanted to: those who recently built or purchased a new house (Deuteronomy 20:5); those who recently started a new business enterprise (Deuteronomy

20:6); those who are engaged to be married (Deuteronomy 20:7); those who have been recently married (Deuteronomy 24:5); and those who are afraid (Deuteronomy 20:8).

It is simply amazing how kind, gracious, wonderful, and wise God, who gave us His perfect Law, is! God cares so much about the prosperity and enjoyment of newlyweds, engaged couples, and those who have acquired houses and businesses, that He is not willing to allow their happiness to be destroyed even in times of national emergency. After all, the whole purpose of fighting for the nation in the first place is to protect these things. Time and again throughout this study, we have seen that God has established His Law with perfect wisdom and understanding for *our benefit* because He cares about us so much. If we obey His Law, we too can be wise and understanding and will have great cause to rejoice.

SLAVERY TO THE LENDER

Another form of slavery generally forbidden by the Law of God is debt-slavery. As disruptive as it would be to the modern economy, a Christian nation must abolish all interest-taking and most collateral-taking for personal loans made to the poor who reside in the nation, and to citizens of the nation. This would include loans for houses, cars, and education among many other things. It would effectively destroy the business models of payday loan companies, credit card companies, home and auto loan companies, some banks, and many, many, businesses which make a large percentage of their profits from predatory financing. However, to obey the Law of God, protect the citizens of the nation from godless money lenders who destroy their lives, and ensure that the nation is truly economically prosperous, the government must put an end to the charging of interest on loans and the taking of collateral in most circumstances. There are many passages throughout the Bible which speak about this issue.

LAWS FORBIDDING THE COLLECTION OF INTEREST

First, it can firmly be established from the Bible that interest-taking is unlawful on personal loans that are issued to any citizen of the nation or any poor person who resides in the nation. Deuteronomy 23:19-20 states,

> You shall not charge interest to your countrymen: interest on money, food, or anything that may be loaned at interest. You may charge interest to a foreigner, but to your countrymen you shall not charge interest, so that the LORD your God may bless you in all that you undertake in the land which you are about to enter to possess.

If someone is a citizen of a nation, he cannot be charged interest on a loan made to him by another citizen or institution in the nation. From the context of this passage and others which refer to interest-taking, personal loans appear to be primarily in sight here. It does not appear that there is anything wrong with charging interest on business loans. A potential exception to this would be small, one-man or family businesses. In such cases, a loan to that business should almost certainly be treated like a personal loan. Loans with interest can also be issued to well-off foreigners who are residing in the nation, and any foreign person or business living outside the nation. Since these loans are unnecessary and very risky, charging interest is perfectly acceptable.

Leviticus 25:35-38 says,

> Now in case a countryman of yours becomes poor and his means with regard to you falter, then you are to sustain him, like a stranger or a sojourner, that he may live with you. Do not take usurious interest from him, but revere your God, that your countryman may live with you. You shall not give him your silver at interest, nor your food for gain. I am the LORD your God, who brought you out of the land of Egypt to give you the land of Canaan and to be your God.

This verse doubles-down on the requirement to not charge interest, especially if your countryman is poor. It is unlawful to charge interest to any of your countrymen, but it is a much more serious offense to charge interest to a poor countryman. However, it also implies that interest cannot be charged on loans made to poor foreigners who are residing in your community. Your poor countrymen are to be sustained through charitable giving and loans without interest like a foreign family who lives in your midst, who you are already doing this for.

This passage also asserts that those who have the means to support the poor are morally obligated by God to help them by interest-free loans. This effectively makes loans made to the poor another form of charitable giving. Accordingly, this means that the well-off should only lend what they are willing to completely lose and, functionally, make into a donation. This is exactly what Jesus admonished us to do in Luke 6:35, when he said, “lend, expecting nothing in return.”

Exodus 22:25 affirms, “If you lend money to My people, to the poor among you, you are not to act as a creditor to him; you shall not charge him interest.” God does not want the rich to become loan sharks, their fear of losing money causing them to mistreat the poor. Rather, He wants them to lend to the poor, expecting nothing in return, because they fear God, love their neighbor, and desire eternal rewards from God.

The Law specifies no civil punishment that would allow the government to force the well-off to give to those in need. However, those who refuse fail to receive the blessings of God, and why would anyone not want God's blessings? Psalm 15:1 asks, "O LORD, who may abide in Your tent? Who may dwell on Your holy hill?" One qualification of a person who will abide in God's tent and on His holy hill is, "he does not put out his money at interest," and we are told he will "never be shaken" (Psalm 15:5). On the other hand, those who refuse to be liberal with what God has given them will be cursed by other men (Proverbs 11:26) and, if they are so greedy for gain that they oppress the poor by charging interest on loans to them, this offense will be seen as an abomination to God and may factor into His decision to end their lives prematurely (Ezekiel 18:13).

LAWS FORBIDDING COLLATERAL-TAKING

The Law is also clear that collateral generally cannot be taken from the poor. Through no fault of their own, there is significant risk that the poor will not be able to pay back loans that are made to them and if this happens, taking collateral from them could be extremely grievous to them and could even cost them their lives. Exodus 22:26 states,

> If you ever take your neighbor's cloak as a pledge, you are to return it to him before the sun sets, for that is his only covering; it is his cloak for his body. What else shall he sleep in? And it shall come about that when he cries out to Me, I will hear him, for I am gracious.

Although collateral may be temporarily taken from the poor as a surety for a loan, it must be returned as soon as they need it. Deuteronomy 24:6 adds, "No one shall take a handmill or an upper millstone in pledge, for he would be taking a life in pledge." In ancient Israel, these tools were used to prepare food, making it difficult for a poor person to live if they were taken away. For this reason, taking things like a stove, refrigerator, home, farm, workspace, small family-run business, car, medication or medical supplies, work tools, phone, computer, or clothing as collateral from poor people should be strictly off-limits in a nation which is obedient to God's Law.

Who is considered poor? In Nehemiah 5:5, the rich were condemned for taking away the fields and vineyards of their poor Jewish brothers, so "poor" does not only refer to those who are homeless, without property, jobless, impoverished, or absolutely destitute; it also refers to anyone who is a middle-class commoner in the nation, even if they own a small business enterprise like a farm or vineyard.

Furthermore, Deuteronomy 24:10-11 states,

> When you make your neighbor a loan of any sort, you shall not enter his house to take his pledge. You shall remain outside, and the man to whom you make the loan shall bring the pledge out to you.

If someone defaults on a personal loan, God's Law does not permit creditors to force entrance into the home of the person to whom the loan was given in order to secure acceptable types of pledged collateral. The creditor must operate under faith that his neighbor will bring the pledge to him. If the neighbor fails to do this, he may have legitimate reasons for why he was unable to make payments and cannot give the collateral to the creditor immediately. Or, if he does not have good reasons and is acting like a thief, this scheme will not work more than once, since this action will affect his reputation with future potential creditors, who will surely take note.

Even if he is acting like a thief, the Law does not permit entry into his home to secure the collateral. Creditors who make personal loans to the poor and to citizens of the nation should only lend what they are willing to lose and must consider this action first and foremost as gift-giving. If repayment is made, he will be happy. If repayment is not made and he loses everything that he lended, that is what he was planning on anyways.

RESTITUTION

Although the government cannot punish those who refuse to lend and give to the poor, it can and should punish those who charge interest to the poor and their fellow citizens and those who take forbidden collateral from the poor. The proper punishment for these offenses is for the creditor to be required to restore everything they charged in interest and everything they took in collateral. Nehemiah 5:1-13 tells a story which illustrates this principle:

> Now there was a great outcry of the people and of their wives against their Jewish brothers. For there were those who said, "We, our sons and our daughters are many; therefore let us get grain that we may eat and live." There were others who said, "We are mortgaging our fields, our vineyards and our houses that we might get grain because of the famine." Also there were those who said, "We have borrowed money for the king's tax on our fields and our vineyards. Now our flesh is like the flesh of our brothers, our children like their

children. Yet behold, we are forcing our sons and our daughters to be slaves, and some of our daughters are forced into bondage already, and we are helpless because our fields and vineyards belong to others."

Then I was very angry when I had heard their outcry and these words. I consulted with myself and contended with the nobles and the rulers and said to them, "You are exacting usury, each from his brother!" Therefore, I held a great assembly against them. I said to them, "We according to our ability have redeemed our Jewish brothers who were sold to the nations; now would you even sell your brothers that they may be sold to us?" Then they were silent and could not find a word to say. Again I said, "The thing which you are doing is not good; should you not walk in the fear of our God because of the reproach of the nations, our enemies? And likewise I, my brothers and my servants are lending them money and grain. Please, let us leave off this usury. Please, give back to them this very day their fields, their

> vineyards, their olive groves and their houses, also the hundredth part of the money and of the grain, the new wine and the oil that you are exacting from them." Then they said, "We will give it back and will require nothing from them; we will do exactly as you say." So I called the priests and took an oath from them that they would do according to this promise. I also shook out the front of my garment and said, "Thus may God shake out every man from his house and from his possessions who does not fulfill this promise; even thus may he be shaken out and emptied." And all the assembly said, "Amen!" And they praised the LORD. Then the people did according to this promise.

This passage is a stark indictment against nations like the United States which are increasingly consolidating all wealth and power from the poor into the hands of a few bankers and rich individuals. It is clear from the Law and this story in Nehemiah that God does not intend banking and finance to become the most important industry in society, gorge itself on a nation's assets, artificially drive prices up exponentially so that commoners can't afford anything, and turn all of the poor into slaves. There must be strict regulation on lending that is in accordance with the wisdom of God's Law to ensure that this situation is never permitted to happen in a Christian nation.

GOD'S COMING WRATH

Wealthy bankers and creditors have such a strangle-hold on the reins of power in seemingly all the nations of the world that it would be exceedingly difficult for even one nation to break free of their grasp. I confess I am not optimistic it will ever happen. However, we can be comforted in the knowledge that all the rich who have oppressed the poor and refuse to repent of their sins will meet a just end in the last days. James 5:1-3 and 5 prophesies,

> Come now, you rich, weep and howl for your miseries which are coming upon you. Your riches have rotted and your garments have become moth-eaten. Your gold and your silver have rusted;

> and their rust will be a witness against you and will consume your flesh like fire. It is in the last days that you have stored up your treasure! [...] You have lived luxuriously on the earth and led a life of wanton pleasure; you have fattened your hearts in a day of slaughter.

Isaiah 5:8-9 warns,

> Woe to those who add house to house and join field to field, until there is no more room, so that you have to live alone in the midst of the land! In my ears the LORD of hosts has sworn, "Surely, many houses shall become desolate, even great and fine ones, without occupants."

Lastly, Habakkuk 2:6-10 presents a future of frightful judgment for the ungodly rich, especially those who become rich from making loans:

> Will not all of these take up a taunt-song against him, even mockery and insinuations against him and say, "Woe to him who increases what is not his—for how long—and makes himself rich with loans?" Will not your creditors rise up suddenly, and those who collect from you awaken? Indeed,

you will become plunder for them. Because you have looted many nations, all the remainder of the peoples will loot you—because of human bloodshed and violence done to the land, to the town and all its inhabitants. Woe to him who gets evil gain for his house to put his nest on high, to be delivered from the hand of calamity! You have devised a shameful thing for your house by cutting off many peoples; so you are sinning against yourself.

CHAPTER VI

RIGHT TO KEEP AND BEAR WEAPONRY FOR SELF-DEFENSE

In 1942, Adolf Hitler made the following statement when he was discussing the German invasion of Russia:

> The most foolish mistake we could possibly make would be to allow the subject races to possess arms. History shows that all conquerors who have allowed their subject races to carry arms have prepared their own downfall by so doing.[31]

Hitler deprived not only those he conquered of their right to possess arms; he also took this right away from German residents he considered to be members of inferior races. The following is an excerpt from the Nazi Weapons Law of November 11, 1938:

[31] Trevor-Roper, H.R. (2000). *Hitler's Table Talk, 1941-1944: His Private Conversations* (Cameron N. and Stevens R.H., trans.). Pg. 425. Enigma Books. (Original work published 1953).

> Jews are prohibited from acquiring, possessing, and carrying firearms and ammunition, as well as truncheons or stabbing weapons. Those now possessing weapons and ammunition are at once to turn them over to the local police authority. Firearms and ammunition found in a Jew's possession will be forfeited to the government without compensation.[32]

Whether they know it or not, those who push gun control are advocating an ideology that has long been championed by racists and is genocidal to its core. Lest you think I am being hyperbolic and you believe that only the Nazis had racist, genocidal gun control laws, the following are examples of gun control laws in the United States.

Florida's 1825 "An Act to Govern Patrols" stipulated that White citizen patrols "shall enter into all negro houses and suspected places, and search for arms and other offensive or improper weapons, and may

---

[32] Nazi Weapon Law of November 11, 1938. (n.d.). Jews for the Preservation of Firearms Ownership (JPFO). https://jpfo.org/filegen-n-z/NaziLawEnglish.htm

lawfully seize and take away all such arms, weapons, and ammunition."[33]

An 1833 Georgia law stated, "it shall not be lawful for any free person of colour in this state, to own, use, or carry fire arms of any description whatever."[34] Even in 1866 after the end of the Civil War and after slavery had been officially abolished in the United States, Alabama passed legislation as part of its Black Code prohibiting Black people from owning firearms or any deadly weapon and forbidding "any person to sell, give, or lend fire-arms or ammunition of any description whatever" to Black people.[35]

Although gun control laws are not always racist, they are always designed to make civilians vulnerable, which is why racist governments love gun control laws. Oftentimes, those who push gun control have nefarious motives (i.e., Hitler desired to take away firearms from civilians so that he could oppress them). Such individuals are textbook examples of oppressors who want to take

---

[33] Ekwall, S. (n.d.). The Racist Origins of US Gun Control: Laws Designed To Disarm Slaves, Freedmen, And African-Americans. The Black Holocaust Society. http://www.blackwallstreet.freeservers.com/gun%20control.htm
[34] Ibid.
[35] Ibid.

advantage of the poor and get vengeance on those who they despise.

On the other hand, many foolish individuals aid these oppressors by supporting gun control laws out of ignorance, believing that weapons, not people, kill people and that it is a good thing for civilians to be dependent on the government for protection. They fully trust that the government will be able to protect them and that the government always has their best interests in mind. This runs contrary to the wisdom found in Psalm 146:3, which says, "Do not trust in princes, in mortal man, in whom there is no salvation." Because of their unwavering trust in the government (which frequently borders on idolatry), individuals who support gun control laws out of ignorance help brutal tyrants oppress their poorest neighbors.

SELL YOUR SUIT AND BUY A GLOCK

For these reasons, and because the Word of God plainly indicates that owning, bearing, and using weapons for the legitimate defense of self or others is lawful, Christian nations should ensure that these rights are protected for everyone in the nation. The first text that clearly indicates this is Luke 22:35-38, which says,

> And He [Jesus] said to them, "When I sent you out without money belt and bag and sandals, you did not lack anything, did you?" They said, "No, nothing." And He said to them, "But now, whoever has a money belt is to take it along, likewise also a bag, and whoever has no sword is to sell his coat and buy one. For I tell you that this which is written must be fulfilled in Me, 'and he was numbered with transgressors'; for that which refers to Me has its fulfillment." They said, "Lord, look, here are two swords." And He said to them, "It is enough."

There are some non-controversial facts which can be ascertained from this passage in support of the right to self-defense. Jesus gave these instructions to his disciples near the very end of his ministry when a mood shift was beginning to happen in Israel. Up until this time, Jesus and His disciples had been "rock stars" in Israel who, although hated by the elites, were loved by the masses. Because of this, all their needs were provided for. Food, money, clothing, and protection were all given to the disciples by the people. However, Jesus knew that things were about to change so the prophecies about Him could be fulfilled. Jesus and His disciples were about to be numbered among the transgressors and hated by everyone except for the elect. So Jesus warned His disciples that, from this point forward, they would need to supply their own money, provisions, and weapons for protection.

From this story, we can establish that it is lawful under the Law of God for civilians to own weapons and use them for protection. Since Jesus gave this right to His disciples, Christian nations ought to follow the example of Jesus and honor this right for those who reside in their nations.

Those who disagree with this claim point out that, shortly after this story, Peter used a sword in an attempt to prevent Jesus from being arrested and our Lord said, "Put your sword back into its place; for all those who take up the sword shall perish by the sword" (Matthew 26:52). However, this statement cannot be isolated from its context to say that all usage of weapons and lethal force is forbidden, otherwise it would contradict other clear commands from God that say the sword must be used for certain reasons (e.g., Romans 13:4 and Genesis 9:6). In context, Jesus was telling Peter that the sword could not be used in this specific instance because it would prevent the prophecies from being fulfilled (Matthew 26:54) and also because it is a generally true statement that rebels who live by the sword (which Peter would have been if he managed to kill a soldier and escape) end up dying by the sword. But it has nothing to do with self-defense or usage of the sword by government ministers.

If it is inherently sinful for civilians to own, bear, or use weapons, then why did Jesus instruct his disciples to acquire them? In modern parlance, Jesus said, “Sell your suit and buy a Glock.” Could Jesus have ever instructed his disciples to “sell your coat and hire a prostitute?” No, because that would be sinful. The fact that Jesus instructed his disciples to acquire swords and approved of it when they showed him the swords they already had clearly indicates it is morally lawful for a civilian to possess weapons. Furthermore, as discussed previously, governments should not outlaw things which are morally lawful and, when they do, these governments are transgressing the role given to them by God in Romans 13.

NO SWORD-CONTROL LAWS IN ANCIENT ISRAEL

Although this story from the New Testament should be enough to establish the requirement for Christian nations to protect the right to possess and use weapons for self-defense, there are several other passages in the Old Testament which make this even clearer. Nehemiah 4:11-14 tells the story of Jews who were rebuilding the walls of Jerusalem when they were threatened by their enemies:

> Our enemies said, "They will not know or see until we come among them, kill them and put a stop to the work." When the Jews who lived near them came and told us ten times, "They will come up against us from every place where you may turn," then I stationed men in the lowest parts of the space behind the wall, the exposed places, and I stationed the people in families with their

> swords, spears and bows. When I saw their fear, I rose and spoke to the nobles, the officials and the rest of the people: "Do not be afraid of them; remember the Lord who is great and awesome, and fight for your brothers, your sons, your daughters, your wives and your houses."

Nehemiah 4:18 also adds, "As for the builders, each wore his sword girded at his side as he built."

There are some interesting things to unpack here. First, it is worth noting that there were no "sword control laws" mentioned here. There are no positive references to weapons control laws found anywhere in the Bible. The only time weapons control is mentioned occurs in 1 Samuel 13:19-22, when the wicked Philistines prohibit the Israelites from acquiring swords, but this furthers my point by showing that these laws are always used to oppress. Unless they were being oppressed by an evil foreign empire, Israelite civilians, like the ones mentioned in the book of Nehemiah, were permitted to own swords, spears, and bows and, apparently, could take these weapons wherever they pleased. There is no indication that any location was ever a "sword free zone."

Even though this appears to have been the policy through the entirety of ancient Israel's history whenever the nation was not subdued by an oppressive foreign power, no issues seem to have ever arisen from this policy. There is no record of the Israelites ever being in fear because of all their Israelite neighbors who carried weapons everyday and there is not a single story or teaching in the Bible where crime is blamed on weapons instead of people (once again shattering the myth that ancient people were more stupid than modern people).

Indeed, it is quite plausible that ancient Israelites lived in less fear of crime than perpetually anxious modern people, precisely because of the fact that almost everyone owned and carried weapons. If it is wrong for civilians to own and bear weapons anywhere and without regulation, why did God not condemn Israel for this, when it was a constant part of life throughout the nation's history? Why are no negative consequences attributed to this policy at any point in the Bible?

A RIGHT AND OBLIGATION TO DEFEND

Another important thing to note is the command in Nehemiah 4:14 to "fight for your brothers, your sons, your daughters, your wives and your houses." This verse establishes, at a minimum, that it is morally acceptable for civilians to use weapons to defend their families and even their private property. 1 Timothy 5:8 also says, "But if anyone does not provide for his own, and especially for those of his household, he has denied the faith and is worse than an unbeliever." Undoubtedly, an important part of providing for your family includes providing for their protection. Therefore, we can conclude that Christian men and women are not just permitted, but are morally obligated to acquire weapons and learn how to use them if that would be the best way to protect their families.

Because of these verses, governments should never pass laws which forbid civilians from protecting their families and property with weapons (either by preventing civilians from owning weapons or by preventing them from carrying these weapons), since this is morally permissible for them and, in the case of protecting their families, is a moral obligation.

Not only should governments refrain from making laws infringing on these rights, but they should actively work to promote the ability of civilians to own, carry, and safely and lawfully use arms. Governments should prevent businesses from making their workplaces and public spaces gun free zones, which effectively deprives men and women of their right to defend themselves and their families' lives almost everywhere outside of the home. Although businesses should generally be allowed to operate without interference from the government, when the business attempts to deprive citizens of their rights—including the God-given right to use weapons to defend themselves and their families—the government must intervene.

In the interest of protecting the nation from crime and foreign invasions, governments should also consider providing high quality weapons training and unarmed self-defense training to their civilians. Furthermore, if a nation has enough resources, firearms and ammunition should be provided to all civilians. These weapons should be the property of the national government, meaning that they can't be sold by the civilian who is borrowing it or taken outside of the nation without the permission of the government. This expenditure is justified as a matter of national defense, which should be a top priority for any national government. The more people in a nation who are heavily armed and know how to use weapons, the more difficult it will be for an oppressive foreign nation to invade. It will also make committing crime much more difficult, since it is harder for criminals to oppress people who have guns. The provision of weapons by the government should in no way restrict the individual's ability to purchase additional weapons.

SELF DEFENSE, NOT OFFENSE

Lastly, although a government must ensure that the right to keep and bear weapons and practice self-defense is firmly established, it must also ensure that this right is never abused to take human life when it is unnecessary or unjust. Exodus 22:2-3 states,

> If the thief is caught while breaking in and is struck so that he dies, there will be no bloodguiltiness on his account. But if the sun has risen on him, there will be bloodguiltiness on his account. He shall surely make restitution; if he owns nothing, then he shall be sold for his theft.

In other words, a person can only kill another human if they are reasonably afraid for their life. If someone breaks into your house in the middle of the night, you may be justified in killing them; you have good reason to think that your life is in danger. However, if someone steals your car from your driveway in broad daylight and you can see they pose no threat to your life, you cannot run outside with your AR-15 and light up the car, killing the thief. That would be an unjust punishment for a property crime.

You are permitted to defend your property with your weapon (Nehemiah 4:14) by having it on you (which may be a deterrent to the criminal) and by then telling the thief to stop or to leave; but you cannot use your weapon to kill the thief in this situation unless you are truly in fear for your life. If you tell the thief to stop and he attempts to pull his own gun on you, at that point you may be justified in shooting him. In a nation which is obedient to God's Law, the government must ensure that no one uses his weapon to carry out excessive, unjust, or vigilante punishments which fall outside the parameters prescribed by the Law.

CHAPTER VII

EQUAL RIGHT TO LIFE

Probably the most fundamental human right protected by the Law is the right to life for all innocent human beings from conception to natural death. Although the issue of abortion is of significant concern, as it is the primary way this right is violated in the world today, it is certainly not the only way this right has been disregarded today or throughout history. Some examples of actual or proposed violations of the right to life include the murder of disabled and genetically inferior people by the Nazis; the allowance and encouragement of assisted suicide in Canada; Pastor Joel Webbon's advocacy for gunning down immigrants, who are made in the image of God, at the border to make an example of them;[36] and the murder

[36] Mantyla, K. (2024, November 14). 'They Need To Be Killed': Joel Webbon Says Anyone Trying To Cross The Border Must Be Shot. People for the American Way. https://www.peoplefor.org/rightwingwatch/they-need-be-killed-joel-webbon-says-anyone-trying-cross-border-must-be-shot

of millions of Armenian Christians by the Ottoman Empire because of their ethnicity and religion.

THE IMAGE OF GOD DOESN'T EXPIRE

The disregard for this most basic of human rights knows no political bounds, as it is frequently transgressed by members of both the Right and the Left. For instance, Andrew Isker, a right-wing Christian political influencer, had this to say on his podcast:

> It's like two-hundred billion dollars a year on kidney dialysis in the United States. Two-hundred billion… like, taxpayers spend that, not people out of pocket. Two-hundred billion dollars. […] Two-hundred dollars, kidney dialysis. You know who needs kidney dialysis? You know, not twenty-three-year-olds, for the most part. It's old people. Right? Um, I mean other than the like random case of somebody whose got like kidney disease as a child. It's for old people. All the stuff that we could do… all the medical spending. The reason why healthcare is twenty percent of the

> American economy… you think that's "the free market! The free market!" No! Absolutely not! Right? We are robbing future generations to keep the old people alive another year or two.[37]

Humans have intrinsic value because we are made in God's image (Genesis 1:27) and because we are so precious to God that He died for us to purchase us (1 Corinthians 6:20, 7:23, Ephesians 1:14, and 2 Peter 2:1). We do not lose this intrinsic value because we haven't been born yet. God masterfully forms our bodies in the womb (Psalm 139:13-16) and even gives emotions to these precious preborn children (Luke 1:44). We also do not lose this intrinsic value because we are old, on kidney dialysis, and only have a few days to live. Such people are equally as valuable in God's sight as a newborn baby or an adult in his prime. We must not flippantly disregard the right to life of these old men and women and refuse to provide for them, because God still cares about these humans who He has made in His image. He will never cut

---

[37] Williams, P. (2025, June 26). *"Pro-life" Christian nationalist pastor Andrew Isker (@BonifaceOption) - from Jackson County TN - outraged about taxpayer money being spent to "keep…* [Post with video from Andrew Isker's show]. X. https://x.com/PhilNvestigates/status/1938416759763259711

off their support for them, so neither should we. As Isaiah 46:4 promises,

> Even to your old age I will be the same, and even to your graying years I will bear you! I have done it, and I will carry you; and I will bear you and I will deliver you.

As God's beloved, it is an abomination for the life of any man to be taken, through action (e.g., shooting someone) or willful neglect (e.g., depriving someone of medical care), except with the express permission of God. Such an action is only permissible for a minister of the state executing just punishment for a heinous crime or for anyone who must kill an aggressor to defend the life of himself or another innocent party. But, all other taking of human life, regardless of whether someone is young, old, or has a physical or mental illness, is a horrendous offense in the eyes of God that is worthy of capital punishment. In Genesis 9:6, God commands, "Whoever sheds man's blood, by man his blood shall be shed, for in the image of God He made man." All human life is so precious to God that the only suitable punishment for the unjust, intentional taking of it is death.

Can We Really Murder Children Because They May Be Unhappy in the Future?

All of this also applies to the detestable practice of murdering another human because of the belief that he or she will have a miserable future. For instance, Corey Mahler, responding to a post commemorating the 80th anniversary of Nazi Propaganda Minister Joseph Goebbels murdering his children and committing suicide because he did not want to live in a world without Hitler, stated, "This was his Christian duty under those circumstances. If you do not understand this fact, then you are no man and should remain silent."[38]

In response to a minister who critiqued Mahler's vile statement, Wesley Todd, co-host of Joel Webbon's Right Response Ministries podcast, commented, "It's a tragic situation but I would do the same if my family was

---

[38] Mahler, C. (2025, May 1). *This was his Christian duty under those circumstances. If you do not understand this fact, then you are no man...* [Post]. X. https://x.com/CoreyJMahler/status/1918006063456240047

going to brutalized [sic] by the red army."[39] When Todd was confronted that he was using the same logic as those who advocate for abortion based on future suffering, he doubled down by saying, "There's a difference between hypothetical suffering and imminent, guaranteed brutality [and] death."[40]

So to avoid the Red Army murdering the Goebbels children, was Joseph Goebbels justified in murdering them himself? Because of Goebbel's devotion to Hitler and his unwillingness to live in a world without him, Goebbels refused an opportunity given to him by Hitler to escape with his family and surrender to the Americans, where his children would have been unharmed, as evidenced by the children of many other Nazi leaders who surrendered to the United States, like Heinrich Himmler's daughter Gudrun and Hermann Göring's daughter Edda. Even if this was not the case, however, no amount of potential future suffering justifies murdering another image bearer of God.

---

[39] Todd, W. (2025, May 1). *It's a tragic situation but I would do the same if my family was going to brutalized by the red...* [Post]. X. https://x.com/Wesley_Todd_/status/1918043047390032378

[40] Todd, W. (2025, May 1). There's a difference between hypothetical suffering and imminent, guaranteed brutality + death. [Post]. X. https://x.com/Wesley_Todd_/status/1918159826812621045

Nowhere in God's Law is potential future suffering given as a permissible excuse to kill another human. We do not know the future and therefore cannot be confident that our predictions of future misery for others will come to pass. Furthermore, even if we could know this for sure, God has never expressed that it is His desire for those who will be miserable to be killed. Being in a state of misery does not mean that we lose the God-given right to life.

Killing children because of the belief that they will be miserable is a position that is not just advocated for by those on the extreme Right. This reasoning is also frequently employed by the Left in their defense of abortion, which is the murder of pre-born children. This gruesome practice is the most egregious and common form of violating the human right to life in the Western world. Even in the United States after *Roe v. Wade* was overturned in 2022, abortion remains legal in all 50 states, as of the writing of this book.[41]

Some states now prohibit doctors from performing abortions, but all states allow a mother to perform a

---

[41] State Index. (n.d.) Abolitionists Rising. https://abolitionistsrising.com/states/

self-managed abortion at any stage of her pregnancy (even at full-term). This explains why the abortion pill industry is flourishing and now accounts for 63% of abortions in the United States,[42] as of 2023. In the same year, the U.S. alone murdered an estimated 1,037,000 little image bearers of God, an increase of 11% from 2020,[43] even after *Roe v. Wade* was overturned. Each year, around 73 million of God's children are torn limb from limb, suctioned, scalded, or starved to death and 29% of all pregnancies (61% of unintended pregnancies) end in abortion.[44] All of this happens in the modern "civilized" world and in almost every "Christian" nation.

---

[42] Jones, R. and Friedrich-Karnik, A. (2024, March 19). Medication Abortion Accounted for 63% of All US Abortions in 2023—An Increase from 53% in 2020. Guttmacher Institute. https://www.guttmacher.org/2024/03/medication-abortion-accounted-63-all-us-abortions-2023-increase-53-2020#:~:text=New%20Guttmacher%20Institute%20research%20from,the%20formal%20health%20care%20system.

[43] Abortion in the United States. (2024, June). Guttmacher Institute. https://www.guttmacher.org/fact-sheet/induced-abortion-united-states

[44] Abortion. (2024, May 17). World Health Organization. https://www.who.int/news-room/fact-sheets/detail/abortion

FOOD FOR THE BIRDS

How can a holocaust of this magnitude, in which innocent children are butchered every day with full awareness, protection, and encouragement from their governments, not bring about the wrath of God? The following text from Jeremiah 7:30-34 describes the judgement that God brought on ancient Judah when they participated in the murder of children:

> "For the sons of Judah have done that which is evil in My sight," declares the LORD, "they have set their detestable things in the house which is called by My name, to defile it. They have built the high places of Topheth, which is in the valley of the son of Hinnom, to burn their sons and their daughters in the fire, which I did not command, and it did not come into My mind. Therefore, behold, days are coming," declares the LORD, "when it will no longer be called Topheth, or the valley of the son of Hinnom, but the valley of the Slaughter; for they will bury in Topheth because there is no other place. The dead bodies of this

> people will be food for the birds of the sky and for the beasts of the earth; and no one will frighten them away. Then I will make to cease from the cities of Judah and from the streets of Jerusalem the voice of joy and the voice of gladness, the voice of the bridegroom and the voice of the bride; for the land will become a ruin."

Jeremiah 19:3-9 provides even more detail about this coming judgment:

> "Behold I am about to bring a calamity upon this place, at which the ears of everyone that hears of it will tingle. Because they have forsaken Me and have made this an alien place and have burned sacrifices in it to other gods, that neither they nor their forefathers nor the kings of Judah had ever known, and because they have filled this place with the blood of the innocent and have built the high places of Baal to burn their sons in the fire as burnt offerings to Baal, a thing which I never commanded or spoke of, nor did it ever enter My mind; therefore, behold, days are coming," declares the LORD, "when this place will no

> longer be called Topheth or the valley of Ben-hinnom, but rather the valley of Slaughter. I will make void the counsel of Judah and Jerusalem in this place, and I will cause them to fall by the sword before their enemies and by the hand of those who seek their life; and I will give over their carcasses as food for the birds of the sky and the beasts of the earth. I will also make this city a desolation and an object of hissing; everyone who passes by it will be astonished and hiss because of all its disasters. I will make them eat the flesh of their sons and the flesh of their daughters, and they will eat one another's flesh in the siege and in the distress with which their enemies and those who seek their life will distress them.

This problem is a five-alarm fire for any nation. Although God may not judge them in exactly the same way He punished ancient Judah, they should anticipate judgment in a way that will be uniquely horrifying to them. They should expect their judgment to be even worse than that experienced by ancient Judah, since they have killed incomprehensibly more babies. The nations are right to be afraid of World War III, nuclear bombs, the grid collapsing, pandemics with high death rates, bloody riots and rebellions, police states with no freedom, and murderous, tyrannical dictators, because they deserve all this and more for what they have done. In fact, there are even more horrifying things than these which the nations *should* be afraid of—warned about in these prophetic passages from Jeremiah—that they have not even stopped to consider yet.

Abolishing abortion, without compromise, must be the top priority for any nation which desires to obey God's Law, uphold the human right to life, and avert God's vengeance for the shedding of innocent blood. Almost all the other issues our nations are experiencing are punishments for the sins of the abortion holocaust. Inflation, governmental tyranny, civil unrest, rampant crime, and unnecessary war are all secondary issues which are caused by the primary issue, abortion. Not only are these things punishments for our sin, but they are also a logical progression from this sin: a nation which denies the reality that the pre-born are humans with human rights will deny economic realities and print money into oblivion, causing inflation; a nation which devalues the lives of the pre-born will devalue the lives of its political enemies, immigrants, elderly, and disabled; and a nation which denies freedom to the pre-born will soon deny freedom to everyone else.

All attempts to resolve any secondary issues without addressing the primary issue will be fruitless. If we continue to murder babies, we should not expect God to help us reduce inflation or get rid of authoritarian leaders. If we were able to get rid of a problem like inflation without repentance for our sin, we should expect God to deliver five new problems for every one problem we are able to resolve. To put it simply, we cannot cling to our heinous, gruesome sins and also demand blessings from God. As long as a nation refuses to repent of its mass murder of babies, it can only expect to receive judgment from God.

Nations which tolerate the murder of the pre-born must act now to remove this scourge from their land immediately, without compromise. If they fail to do this they should remember it is likely God will choose not to forgive the blood that they have shed at some point, even if their leaders later try to turn from their sins like King Manesseh did. 2 Kings 24:2-4 warns,

> The LORD sent against him [Jehoiakim] bands of Chaldeans, bands of Arameans, bands of Moabites, and bands of Ammonites. So He sent them against Judah to destroy it, according to the word of the LORD which He had spoken through His servants the prophets. Surely at the command of the LORD it came upon Judah, to remove them from His sight because of the sins of Manasseh, according to all that he had done, and *also for the innocent blood which he shed, for he filled Jerusalem with innocent blood; and the LORD would not forgive.* [emphasis added]

LIFE AT FERTILIZATION

What exactly do I mean by saying that we should "not compromise" with abortion? First, it must be remembered that life begins at fertilization, something that 96% of biologists[45] are in agreement about. The

[45] Jacobs, S. (2021). The Scientific Consensus on When a Human's Life Begins. NIH. https://pubmed.ncbi.nlm.nih.gov/36629778/

moment of fertilization is when a new human being with a unique genetic code that has never existed before and will never exist again comes into existence. All other starting points are arbitrary and can be used to justify a wide range of genocidal human rights abuses outside the womb.

Those who say that babies in the womb aren't alive and don't have human rights because they are not breathing on their own yet cannot explain why adults who are on ventilators are alive and deserve human rights. Those who say that babies in the womb aren't alive and don't have human rights because they aren't sentient can't explain why people in comas are alive and have human rights. Those who say that babies in the womb aren't alive and don't have human rights because their bodies or minds aren't "fully-developed" can't explain why young children are alive and have human rights, since their minds and bodies also are not fully-developed yet. Those who say that babies in the womb aren't alive and don't have human rights because they will be born into poverty or sad circumstances can't explain why poor or depressed adults are alive and have human rights. Scientists are not always right, but in this case they are completely correct that the only logical point at which human life begins is fertilization.

The Bible also confirms that God forms our lives in the womb. Psalm 139:13-18 states,

> For You formed my inward parts; You wove me in my mother's womb. I will give thanks to You, for I am fearfully and wonderfully made; wonderful are Your works, and my soul knows it very well. My frame was not hidden from You, when I was made in secret, and skillfully wrought in the depths of the earth; Your eyes have seen my unformed substance; and in Your book were all written the days that were ordained for me, when as yet there was not one of them. How precious also are Your thoughts to me, O God! How vast is the sum of them! If I should count them, they would outnumber the sand. When I awake, I am still with You.

Likewise, Luke 1:44 records the reaction of Elizabeth (who was pregnant with John the Baptist) when she met Mary, who was pregnant with Jesus: "For behold, when the sound of your greeting reached my ears, the baby leaped in my womb for joy." Only a living being can "leap for joy." If this being is in a human womb, it is a human. Since it is a living human being, it is entitled to human rights. He does not gain or lose these rights because of his size, age, or level of development.

Equal Justice for Equal Humans

Both science and the Bible are clear that babies, from the moment God begins to form them in the womb at fertilization, are just as much human beings as any fully-grown human being. Therefore, killing a developing image bearer of God knowingly, without lawful and moral justification, and with malice aforethought must be treated exactly the same as killing a fully-grown image bearer of God. Exodus 21:22-25 describes this situation in specific detail:

> If men struggle with each other and strike a woman with child so that she gives birth prematurely, yet there is no injury, he shall surely be fined as the woman's husband may demand of

> him, and he shall pay as the judges decide. But if there is any further injury, then you shall appoint as a penalty life for life, eye for eye, tooth for tooth, hand for hand, foot for foot, burn for burn, wound for wound, bruise for bruise.

If someone causes a woman to deliver a baby prematurely, but there is no injury to the child, he or she must make financial restitution to the parents of the child as directed by the parents and the court. However, if someone causes injury that results in the death of the child in the womb, they will pay for it with their life. Any other injuries that they cause to the child that are non-fatal, they will be punished in the same way assault charges must be punished for any victim who is outside the womb. Under God's Law, justice for children in the womb is fair and impartial.

INCREMENTAL PRO-LIFE LEGISLATION

If someone murders another image bearer of God, regardless of the victim's size, level of development, location, age, level of dependence or independence, gender, race, or mental or physical handicaps, the murderer must be punished in the same way as anyone else. Allowing any image bearer of God to be murdered (or refusing to justly punish the murderer) on account of one of the previously described characteristics is sinful partiality, condemned by James 2:9. If your nation or state has a law that tolerates the murder of an image bearer up to her birth, that is an abomination to God. Likewise, if your nation or state has a law that tolerates the murder of an image bearer up to her ninth week of existence, that is also an abomination to God.

Unlike God, the pro-life establishment in the United States does make a distinction based on gestational age. Many pro-life activists and politicians assert that, by creating laws that restrict some abortions, they will eventually find themselves in a position to outlaw all abortion. Although these people claim to be against abortion, the laws they create—such as heartbeat laws—give state protection for *some* abortions. This "incremental" pro-life legislation which tolerates the murder of some of God's children (whether they are twenty-four weeks old or six weeks old) is never a victory; it protects the murder of a class of humans based on their age and size, which is sinful partiality and forbidden in no uncertain terms by the Law of God.

Incremental pro-life laws which forbid mothers who murder their babies from being prosecuted have the effect of keeping abortion legal. If a nation had a law against murder with the caveat that one class of people could not be prosecuted for murdering another class of people (e.g., if White people could not be prosecuted for murdering Black people), that law would effectively make the murder of those people legal, would be sinfully partial, and would be an abomination to God. It simply does not matter whether or not these laws are an improvement from previous laws because they are equally abominable to God. God is as displeased when a forty-week-old baby is murdered as He is when a five-week-old baby is murdered.

Leviticus 20:2-5 serves as a terrifying example to nations which tolerate, *to any degree*, those who sacrifice children:

> Any man from the sons of Israel or from the aliens sojourning in Israel who gives any of his offspring to Molech, shall surely be put to death; the people of the land shall stone him with stones. I will also set My face against that man and will cut him off from among his people, because he has given some of his offspring to Molech, so as to defile My sanctuary and to profane My holy name. If the people of the land, however, should ever disregard that man when he gives *any* [emphasis added] of his offspring to Molech, so as not to put him to death, then I Myself will set My face against that man and against his family, and I will cut off from among their people both him and all those who play the harlot after him, by playing the harlot after Molech.

There is no mention here about the size or level of development of the child who is sacrificed. God did not say, "If you tolerate the murder of a five year old, I will set my face against you and cut you off. But, if you tolerate the murder of a smaller, less-developed two year old, then I will give you a pat on the back, because at least you're making incremental progress in the right direction!" All child sacrifice is an abomination to God and those who permit the murder of *any* children at any age, regardless of the excuse (such as, "at least we were moving in the right direction!") have no reason to expect anything other than the fierce opposition of God as exemplified in this passage.

DOES GOD'S TOLERATION OF DIVORCE REALLY MEAN THAT WE CAN TOLERATE THE MURDER OF CHILDREN?

Those who argue for unjust incremental pro-life laws which tolerate some baby murder will frequently cite the fact that God hates divorce (Malachi 2:16) and, yet, God allowed the Israelites to be divorced because of the hardness of their hearts (Matthew 19:8). If God allowed people to divorce their spouses (which He hates), then maybe we should allow people to kill some of their babies (which He also hates), in our pursuit of abolishing abortion. Although this reasoning is commonly used, there are two obvious problems with it.

First, God allowed divorces to happen to prevent hard-hearted spouses from murdering each other—something objectively worse than divorce, even though divorce is awful. God is primarily concerned about preventing *murder*. But the pro-life incrementalist uses this command as an excuse to tolerate murder!

Second, we are not God. God can choose to instruct governments to allow some divorces because He has perfect foreknowledge and knows it will serve the purposes of His good will, even though He hates divorce. We cannot choose to instruct governments to allow some murders, rapes, or child sexual abuse, because we are not God, we do not have perfect foreknowledge, and we do not have authority to override His commands.

If Christians started to gain control of a perverted nation which legally tolerated the sexual abuse of children, would it be an incremental "victory" to pass a law which made it illegal to have sex with minors between the ages of twelve and sixteen, but still allowed adults to have sex with children under the age of twelve?

Using the same logic they use to defend the toleration of some baby murder, pro-life incrementalists would be obligated to say that this law would be an incremental "victory." But this is absurd. All child sexual abuse, regardless of the child's age, is an abomination. *No amount* of child sexual abuse and *no amount* of baby murder (regardless of the victim's age or what was formerly tolerated in society) is acceptable under the Law of God.

Furthermore, although divorces specifically are tolerated in the Law in some instances (Deuteronomy 24:1), murder is never tolerated in the Law or anywhere in the Word of God. Exodus 20:13 says, "You shall not murder." It does not say, "You shall not murder, unless it is part of an incremental plan to save the most number of lives possible. Then some murder is tolerable in the meantime."

Deuteronomy 27:19 says, "Cursed is he who distorts the justice due an alien, orphan, and widow." It does not say, "Cursed is he who distorts the justice due an alien, orphan, and widow; however, if you allow justice to be distorted for some orphans (whose parents want to kill them) for a time while you shore up political support for future incremental pieces of legislation, then you will not be cursed."

Jeremiah 22:3 says, "Do not mistreat or do violence to the stranger, the orphan, or the widow; and do not shed innocent blood in this place." It does not say, "Do not mistreat or do violence to the stranger, the orphan, or the widow; and do not shed innocent blood in this place. But, some violence against the smallest and youngest orphans is okay and it is fine to shed their innocent blood in this place, as long as you promise that you are working on a solution to end this problem some day in the future."

Psalm 82:3 says, "Vindicate the weak and fatherless." It does not say, "Vindicate the weak and fatherless; however, it is acceptable to not vindicate some of the fatherless if it will help you accomplish your political goals and ambitions."

The point here is that the Bible never says that murder can be tolerated for any reason. Murder is always wrong, no matter the excuse.

MOSTLY ACCEPTABLE TO GOD

Another objection presented by incrementalists comes from verses like 2 Kings 15:34-35, which states,

> [King Jotham] did what was right in the sight of the LORD; [...] Only the high places were not taken away; the people still sacrificed and burned incense on the high places.

Essentially, they argue if King Jotham could still be considered a generally "good" king who did what was right in the sight of the Lord even though he tolerated some sin in his kingdom, it must be possible for there to be a "good" magistrate today who tolerates some baby murder. This is an odd argument. King Jotham was not perfect and allowed some idolatry to occur in his kingdom and these incrementalists want to emulate the things that he did wrong? Why not try to be perfect, as our heavenly Father is perfect (Matthew 5:48)? "Good enough" should never be in the vocabulary of a Christian, especially when it comes to heinous sins like the butchering of babies.

Yes, in some sense, kings like Jotham did a lot of good and God, because He is just, wanted to give these kings credit where credit was due. But He specifically recorded their sins so that, for all human history, we would remember that God still takes issue with kings like Jotham. If you are a saint of God who desires to be a good magistrate or a good voter, why would you be okay with God having something against you in the history books?

LESSER OF TWO EVILS?

When it comes to voting, I do actually believe these stories about the kings of Judah are a powerful argument for Christians being able to vote for the comparative lesser of two evils. If God was able to express some level of approval for an Old Testament king who generally did what was good compared to other exceptionally wicked kings, but who allowed the high places to remain, I think it also would have been permissible for God's people to express their approval for them by voting for these kings.

However, if it is *ever* possible for someone to sin by casting a vote for some law or some person, it is *certainly* sinful for a person to vote to protect the mass murder of babies or for rulers who say that they will do this, since this is one of the worst forms of evil imaginable. There are some evils which are so gross that we can *never* vote for them or anyone who advocates for them. If this is not true for abortion, it is not true for anything. If someone must choose between voting for one of two candidates who have both vowed to protect child sacrifice, he should vote for neither; if he votes for either, thereby knowingly expressing his support for the murder of children, regardless of his excuse, Leviticus 20:2-5 indicates that God will hold him responsible, unless he repents.

"But one candidate is going to kill more babies than the other!" This is a textbook example of utilitarian ethical thinking which is anti-Christian. *All* baby murder is incredibly evil. God is very displeased with someone who murders (or consents to murder) even one baby. If someone murders (or consents to murder) a thousand babies, He of course will be even more displeased. But He is not going to give someone a pat on the back and say, "Good for you, only consenting to murder five-hundred babies instead of a thousand!" If someone murders or consents to murder even just one baby, he merits God's righteous wrath against him.

"But one political candidate wants to protect late term abortions and the other does not!" This is yet another example of anti-Christian utilitarian thinking and is an objection that should never come out of the mouth of someone who truly believes that *all* human beings are equally valuable and made in the image of God. Is God pleased when a serial killer decides to stop murdering people over the age of 30 and only murders people under the age of 30 instead? Would He be pleased with governing authorities or voters who decided to reduce the age of legalized serial killing from 40 to 30, so that they could feel a little bit better about themselves? Of course not.

Why is baby murder a sin that Christian magistrates and voters can never compromise with? In addition to the previous Bible passages which have been brought up (most importantly, Leviticus 20:1-5, which warns that God will cut off *all* those who disregard the murder of babies), there are many examples in the Old Testament of nations and kings who actually practiced child sacrifice and God *never* said anything good about these people while they were committing this sin. In Judah, there are two recorded instances of specific kings who participated in child sacrifice and, in both instances, God was fiercely angry with these kings because of this.

2 Kings 16:2-3 states,

> Ahaz was twenty years old when he became king, and he reigned sixteen years in Jerusalem; and he did not do what was right in the sight of the LORD his God, as his father David had done. But he walked in the way of the kings of Israel, and even made his son pass through the fire, according to the abominations of the nations whom the LORD had driven out from before the sons of Israel.

Additionally, 2 Kings 21:6 says,

> He [King Manesseh] made his son pass through the fire, practiced witchcraft and used divination, and dealt with mediums and spiritists. He did much evil in the sight of the LORD provoking Him to anger.

If someone is an unrepentant magistrate or voter who knowingly engages in, protects, supports, or consents to child sacrifice, it is safe to assume that these verses describe him. "James Smith sacrificed babies and did much evil in the sight of the Lord, provoking Him to anger. He did not do what was right in the sight of the Lord his God." For those who turn to God in repentance, God will forgive their sins, even very gross ones such as the murder of children, like He did with King Manasseh (2 Chronicles 33:10-20). They (and their nations) may still suffer extreme consequences in this life for their horrific sin of bloodshed (2 Kings 24:4), but God will completely forgive them in the eternal sense. However, no Christian should ever want to have the legacy Manasseh had.

THE WILLIAM WILBERFORCE WAY

Lastly, incrementalists frequently cite William Wilberforce, a Christian who led the movement to abolish slavery in England—which occured incrementally over the course of about twenty years—as an example of the success and virtue of incrementalist policies. This is the easiest objection to deal with, because William Wilberforce had something to say about this issue in his *A Letter on the Abolition of the Slave Trade* which also serves as an excellent conclusion to this chapter. Although his writing is a bit dense and archaic, it is greatly relevant to the present debate. Referring to his political opponents who supported the gradual (incremental) abolition of the slave trade, Wilberforce stated,

> Let me be forgiven if I speak strongly, where I feel so very deeply. It is not only because *the gradual Abolitionists have been, in fact, the only real stay on that system of wickedness and cruelty which we wish to abolish; though that assertion is unquestionably true; but it is trying beyond expression that they should be the real maintainers of the Slave Trade* [emphasis added], who reprobate it in terms of detestation as strong as any which we ourselves can utter. Nor do I mean (the declaration is made with solemnity and truth) that these expressions are not sincere. If they were not proved to be so by the general character of those

who use them, my personal knowledge of some of them, and the esteem and regard I entertain for them, excludes the contrary supposition. Yet I cannot but believe, that, could they have clearly foreseen what would be the practical effect of their opposition, it would not have been continued for an hour.

Let them now, however, remember the grounds and principles on which they resisted our measure; that they themselves stated the question to be only between two different modes of abolishing the Slave Trade. [...]

But the gradual Abolitionists chiefly urged, that we were too hasty and violent, and that by our precipitancy we should defeat our own purpose [emphasis added]. For, without the concurrence of the colonial legislatures, it was alleged, we could not carry our measure into effect; they advised that time, therefore, should be allowed for softening the prejudices and cooling the warmth of the colonists.

What has followed since that period? *The Slave Trade, instead of eight, has now lasted fourteen years* [emphasis added]. Far more time, therefore, has been allowed the Planters for completing their gangs, than was originally proposed by any one who did not avow himself a friend to the perpetuity of the Slave Trade. A far greater number of Slaves, also, than was then in any one's contemplation, has since been imported [...]

Let me also remind these gentlemen, that if we immediate Abolitionists conceive them, *the gradual Abolitionists, to be, though unintentionally, the real practical friends and supporters of the Slave Trade* [emphasis added], we at least are not the only persons who hold that opinion. The West Indians, who frankly declare they never can consent to the abolition, nay even the Slave Traders themselves, evidently shew that they conceive these gradual Abolitionists to be their real adherents. Against them ought to have been directed the objects of derision and contempt.

We were a set of well-meaning visionaries, who were proposing what, even if carried into effect, would be found utterly impracticable. Whereas they were men of sound practical understanding, who had wisdom to devise effectual measures for executing all which their virtue might suggest. This is not urged with levity, it is seriously and earnestly pressed. Nor is it a statement without instruction. It has often been justly urged, that we may collect much as to the character of any man, or the tendency of any measure, by observing them not only in themselves, but, when that investigation is difficult and doubtful, *by observing who are their enemies and who are their friends. Tried by this principle at least, we know that judgement would be passed on the gradual Abolitionists* [emphasis added]."[46]

[46] Wilberforce, W. (1807). *A Letter on the Abolition of the Slave Trade*. Pg. 94-97. No publisher.

CONCLUSION

Oftentimes, we find ourselves asking the same question that the Psalmist asks in Psalm 8:3-4,

> When I consider Your heavens, the work of Your fingers, the moon and the stars, which You have ordained; what is man that You take thought of him, and the son of man that You care for him?

It is absolutely amazing that the God of the universe has so thoughtfully, exhaustively, and clearly established *universal, equal rights* for mere humans in His Law. Why has He done this? First, because God is no respecter of persons (Romans 2:11) and He does not give us more or fewer rights because of any characteristic. Rather, He gives us equal rights because He made all people equally in His image (Genesis 1:26). Humans are not any more or less made in the image of God because they are young, old, Black, White, Jewish, disabled, male, female, an immigrant, or native-born. Therefore, all have equal rights in the eyes of God and He expects us to imitate Him (Ephesians 5:1) by showing no partiality or favoritism (James 2:9, Deuteronomy 1:17, 16:19, Proverbs 28:21, and 1 Timothy 5:21). For instance, we cannot show partiality to native-born people by affirming that they have human rights and then show partiality against foreigners by denying that they have these same rights. God does not do this and His Law specifically forbids such partiality (Leviticus 19:34).

More importantly, however, God has established universal, equal human rights in His Law because He loves us. God loves all men, regardless of their demographics, so much that He died for them (1 John 2:2). He even loves His enemies (Matthew 5:43-48) and died for them (Romans 5:8). As a part of this love, God desires to ensure that men do not mistreat each other, which is why has established basic human rights which are universally applicable to all humans and which cannot be violated. God wants all humans to have life, liberty, and freedom from the terror of violent, partial men. He has written His Law to safeguard these things and to convict those who freely choose to do evil to their neighbors.

The Law is incomprehensibly wonderful in its care for us. God loves the poor so much that His Law does not permit the rich to force them into debt slavery through exorbitant interest rates (Exodus 22:25). God is so concerned for those who have recently been married that His Law forbids them from going to war (Deuteronomy 24:5). God cares about the pre-born so much that His Law forbids them from being killed because of their age and He awards some of the most severe punishments imaginable to those who commit this sin or support it (Leviticus 20:2-5). God deeply values the elderly and His Law does not allow for them to be murdered through the denial of medical treatment or any other means (Genesis 9:6).

God hears the cry of poor foreigners and His Law ensures that they are treated equally and forbids any violence from being done to them (Leviticus 19:34 and Jeremiah 22:3). God uplifts women and His Law permits them to hold positions of power and influence, like He gave to Deborah (Judges 4-5). God delights in the love of mixed-race couples, like Ruth and Boaz (Ruth 4:13), and His Law protects their right to marry. God wants people to be able to protect themselves from wicked men, so His Law permits men and women to keep and bear weapons for self-defense (Luke 22:36 and Nehemiah 4:13-14).

As we can see, God's Law is very good. Psalm 119:72 says, "The law of Your mouth is better to me than thousands of gold and silver pieces." Psalm 19:7-10 sings,

> The law of the LORD is perfect, restoring the soul; the testimony of the LORD is sure, making wise the simple. The precepts of the LORD are right, rejoicing the heart; the commandment of the LORD is pure, enlightening the eyes. The fear of the LORD is clean, enduring forever; the judgments of the LORD are true; they are righteous altogether. They are more desirable than gold, yes, than much fine gold; sweeter also than honey and the drippings of the honeycomb.

Deuteronomy 4:5-8 proclaims,

> See, I have taught you statutes and judgments just as the LORD my God commanded me, that you should do thus in the land where you are entering to possess it. So keep and do them, for that is your wisdom and your understanding in the sight of the

> peoples who will hear all these statutes and say, "Surely this great nation is a wise and understanding people." For what great nation is there that has a god so near to it as is the LORD our God whenever we call on Him? Or what great nation is there that has statutes and judgments as righteous as this whole law which I am setting before you today?

Lamentably, even though God's Law is perfect (Psalm 19:7) and His commands are not burdensome (1 John 5:3), but bring joy (Psalm 19:8), many men freely choose to disregard God's Law and violate the rights of their neighbors. In the modern era, it has become very common for men to do this because of partisan politics.

People have elevated the beliefs of their political party to a level that should be held only by the Word of God. Right-wingers see Leftists doing evil things and, because of this, they believe it is imperative for them to support everything anyone on the Right believes so they can defeat their shared political enemies. Leftists do the same thing. In so doing, both sides compromise with sin, rebel against God's perfect Law, oppress their neighbors, and become the monsters they complain about.

As we continue to get closer and closer to the end of days, this state of affairs will only grow worse and worse. Matthew 24:12 says, "Because *lawlessness* [emphasis added] is increased, most people's love will grow cold." We see this process playing out every day. Leftists do horrible things which violate God's Law—murdering the pre-born and sexualizing children—causing the love of men on the Right to grow cold. Then, hatred fills this void in the hearts of these men on the Right and some of them start advocating for gunning down immigrants at the border, referring to Jews as "parasites," saying that women shouldn't be seen in public, calling for the use of violence to remove even second and third generation immigrants from society, and praising Hitler as "Christian Prince." Moderate Leftists then see this wicked lawlessness on the Right and become more extreme Leftists, propelling them into greater and greater evil. And the cycle repeats as lawlessness breeds more lawlessness.

But the good news for us is that we can break this cycle, at least in our spheres of influence, by obeying God's Law. We can learn about this Law from studying God's Word from cover to cover and being guided by the Holy Spirit (John 16:13), who writes God's Law on our hearts (Hebrews 10:16). By refusing to participate in the cycle of lawlessness, by showing love to our neighbors, and by protecting their God-given human rights, we can reignite the cold hearts of those around us. In so doing, this will be a delight for us as well, bringing God's blessings on our lives. As Deuteronomy 5:32-33 instructs,

> So you shall observe to do just as the LORD your God has commanded you; *you shall not turn aside to the right or to the left* [emphasis added]. You shall walk in all the way which the LORD your God has commanded you, that you may live and that it may be well with you, and that you may prolong your days in the land which you will possess.

www.ingramcontent.com/pod-product-compliance
Lightning Source LLC
LaVergne TN
LVHW090558110826
845146LV00001B/173